COINCIDENTALLY

COINCIDENTALLY

George William Rutler

A Crossroad Book
The Crossroad Publishing Company
New York

The Crossroad Publishing Company
16 Penn Plaza, 481 Eighth Avenue
Suite 1550
New York, NY 10001

Printed in the United States of America

Library of Congress Cataloging-in-Publication Data

Rutler, George W. (George William)
  Coincidentally / George William Rutler.
      p. cm.
  ISBN-13: 978-0-8245-2440-1 (alk. paper)
  ISBN-10: 0-8245-2440-3 (alk. paper)
  1. Curiosities and wonders—Anecdotes. 2. Coincidence—Anecdotes.
3. History—Anecdotes. 4. Biography—Anecdotes. I. Title.

  AG243.R84 2007
  031.02—dc22

2007006725

1 2 3 4 5 6 7 8 9 10   12 11 10 09 08 07

Dedicated to the memory of Agoracritus
sculptor of the Nemesis of Rhamnus
(Fifth Century, B.C.)

Contents

Contents

Preface

The idea which led to this book came when I was traveling to Stamford, Connecticut on the New Haven Line. As the train rolled past the spires of Larchmont and timeless battlements of Rye, I set about to review the day's mail. One man had written to tell how a certain member of his favorite local basketball team scored the decisive point on a certain day of each month. Upon this fragile frame he had constructed a numerological theory too complex to describe here, but one which got him a front seat next to the coach's wife at a championship game.

Experience had taught me that the letter's length and lack of margins can indicate an unhealthy impatience with convention, or even schizophrenia. I recalled many of the letters like it that I have received: a man in Florida writing monthly to tell how the Book of Revelation ties in with the monetary policies of the World Bank, a woman in a western state claiming that the portents on her rhododendron coincide with her daughters' pregnancies, and an author requesting a cover blurb for his book on how Biblical prophecies shed light on Iraq's military capabilities. I resolved to write an essay showing how innumerable are life's coincidences, and how insignificant they usually are. The more I wrote, the more there was to write, and when I began to write one essay several flowed forth. There is no end to insignificance. Let me give some examples.

Winston Churchill died in the three hundredth anniversary year of the death of Sarah Churchill's friend and nemesis, Queen Anne. It would have been a better coincidence if he had died on the actual date, as Franco died on the very anniversary of the execution of the founder of the Falange, José Antonio Primo de Rivera. More poignant was the death in 1687 of Jean Baptiste Lully from an abscess after striking his foot with a long baton while conducting a Te Deum in thanksgiving for the recovery of Louis XIV from an abscess. In one of the more colorful anecdotes in the pageant of organic chemistry, Friedrich August Kekule von Stradonitz dreamt of a snake curled up into a ring just before he thought up his theory of the ring structure of the benzene molecule. Perhaps the dream inspired the theory, in which case it was not insignificant; or, I think more likely, the dream may have been a subconscious expression of the theory gestating in his mind. Some events have obvious psychological causes, like Kierkegaard collapsing and dying in 1855 on his way home from the bank on the day his trust fund ran out, or General Arthur MacArthur (Douglas's father) dying in 1912 at the fiftieth and final reunion of his beloved regiment, the 24th Wisconsin.

Looking for coincidences can become as contagious as punning, although one trusts that keepers of coincidences are not universally despised the way punsters are. Some untutored protocol requires that every pun should be answered with a groan, but if you point out the least significant coincidence you will often get a gasp of wonder. This may be tribute to an old maxim which holds that coincidences are divine puns.

There have been coincidences too many to name in my own experience and virtually everyone can say the same. I have resolved not to admit to my public repertoire those which are of a personal nature. Meeting one's long-lost and forgotten cousin on Lexington Avenue just after her name had come to mind for no apparent reason, is an interesting event but a private one. So is receiving a letter from an official on the same day you had written to him for the first time in several years, or realizing that the combination numbers on a security lock match the date of the death of Pope Symmachus. One morning a photograph in a college alumni newsletter reminded me of a classmate I had not thought about in thirty-three years, and three hours later he sat down behind me in Christie's at an auction of French bronzes. Upon completing an essay about the Battle of Scinde, I noticed in a cast-off pamphlet that my own grandfather's Cheshire regiment had fought in it. And how can one be invited to lecture in Syracuse, New York on the 212th day of the year and be unmoved by remembrance of 212 B.C., when Archimedes was slain during the sack of Syracuse in Greece? Any respondent can come up with one even better. In the cocktail lounge of a hotel, Franklin Roosevelt's son James introduced himself to a woman and asked if they had met before; she replied that she had once been his wife. James Roosevelt was something of a public person but that encounter was a private matter of limited curiosity, and because of bibulous circumstances it may not have been a coincidence at all.

Of wider moral interest are stories like the one of Henry Ziegland of Honey Grove, Texas, who was shot in 1893. His attacker then killed himself, but Mr. Ziegland had only fainted: the bullet had grazed his head and lodged in a tree. In 1913, while doing some house repairs, Mr. Ziegland dynamited the tree, and the bullet shot straight out and into his head, finally accomplishing its purpose. Scientists will find some portent in the simultaneous discovery of the position of the planet Neptune in 1846, by John Couch Adams in England and Joseph

Leverrier in France. Military historians may note the death of General Henry W. Lawton at the Battle of San Mateo in the Philippines by the troops of Licerio Geronimo, thirteen unlucky years after he had captured the Apache chief Geronimo, who was unrelated to Filipino.

I decided to mention only items that are of universal application, mindful that I speak of universality as a New Yorker, and as one aware that New Yorkers are accused of a myopic vision of the world. I live in the middle of Manhattan, which is the heart of New York, which is the center of the United States, which, in turn, is the focus of the whole planet. "This fragile Earth our island home" as some lame poesie puts it, is the only inhabited planet in the universe as far as we know. That itself seems a very important coincidence. Thus, of the billions of humans alive today, I sleep on a bed which is in the very epicenter of our galaxy. When I mention this in other parts of the world, people receive this defensively as a comment on their life in remote places.

Admittedly, living in the center of things colors my perspective; and my sustained enthusiasm for peripheral subjects is not shared by many. In this connection, I recall a remark of the Irish writer Shane Leslie in the 1920's in his introduction to a book of reminiscences by Archbishop Robert Seton, titular archbishop of Heliopolis. He said that not least among the prelate's charms was his innocent assumption that what interested him would also interest his readers. The thought has crossed my mind from time to time that the guileful might say the same of my own innocence. My first defense is this: I wrote what follows first of all for my own edification, of which I have need. My second defense is more contentious: I cannot expect that multitudes will absorb themselves in this kind of *jeu d'e-sprit* because the present generation's historical taste has faded in the senility of western culture.

While nature has not made me a cheerless person, I am saddened by our age's limited frame of reference. The more money is spent on education, the more do academic standards dwindle and the faster does illiteracy spread. This first causality is literal literacy: today's children are growing up inured to split infinitives, even on the front of *The New York Times*. The plague spreads. Then the general grasp on culture weakens. The burden on schools to teach technologies of all sorts restricts the time available for the grandeurs of the liberal arts and the glories of the races, but these trophies of the ages are not dispensable.

Although I am helpless with computers, to the exasperation of friends who have gone to lengths to show me how to operate them, I should think that a new and less ambisinistrous generation with access to so much computerized information must have an easier job of unearthing deeply moving historical coincidence than I have had. Because of my inadequacy with machines, I have had to rely for the most part on my brain and so have felt somewhat at a disadvantage with researchers who are good at what is called "artificial intelligence." Yet scholarship has not measured up to the new technology. After a lecture at one distinguished university, a freshman asked if the term "Second World War" means that there had been a previous one; and at another well-known school not one member of the graduating class could name a single Duke of Angouleme. The narrowing of cultural references constrains our contemporary views as well. The NBC television network in one recent year broadcast 327 reports on foreign news, down from 1,013 eight years earlier. The problem is not isolationism; it is solipsism. We may communicate more rapidly than ever, and travel more widely, but there is a cultural autism along with it, a disengagement from other people and civilizations.

It does not take a man as clever as Will Rogers to agree with him on a wise and incontestable point: "Everybody is ignorant, only on different subjects." Ignorance now runs wildly beyond anything he could have imagined. Two-thirds of American 17-year olds cannot date the decade of the Civil War because they are too busy dating each other. One-third of them think that Columbus sailed the ocean blue sometime after 1750, which does not even rhyme. Some have told me that I assume too much about what students do know, and I have grown increasingly aware of what they mean. It is more than good, it is highly crucial, for the Pope to have written an encyclical about the need to recover philosophy in our schools, but the next shoe to drop has to be history. The two are in tandem. A particular philosophy will decide whether or not we need history and what kind we need. St. Dionysius said that history is philosophy taught by example, but he meant a mutual obedience to reality. For the nihilist there is no history other than date, and for the ideologue there is no history other than propaganda. That is why the Poles used to say that under Marxism the future is well-known—it is the past that is uncertain. Risking paranoia, I think it will be design and not just neglect that history was squeezed out of the curriculum. If the young are persuaded that all of life is an impression and that truth is opinion, they will not be obedient to fact. There need be no interest in fact. They will not even read tautology in the common term "true fact."

But delicate with them I shall be, as a last remnant of a golden age writing to the chirping fledglings of a new dark age.

The social amnesia to which I have alluded breeds fanaticism, and a sure way to spot fanatics is by their humorlessness. A sense of humor requires a sense of balance, because humor is the perception of imbalance. A fanatic on any subject lacks measure when it comes to writing and speaking: the average speech of Fidel Castro is hours longer than Abraham Lincoln's at Gettysburg. The letters of fanatics run on to many pages after the message has been exhausted. If you tell fanatics a joke, be they right wing or left wing fanatics, they will stare at you with the bewildered look of a dog listening to a whistle in a strange frequency. In this group, I scientifically lump all those who do not appreciate what I say.

It does seem that as eccentricity is a marked characteristic of the English, so is fanaticism an American trait. One of the many facets of Lincoln's genius was his amused perception of absurdity in a time of rampant enthusiasms. The South might have done better if Lee and Davis had shown some of his gift, but neither seems to have been able to lighten up a crowd. Woodrow Wilson had the same problem. Lincoln was at least as righteous as Wilson, but Lincoln also was right more than Wilson. Wilson's utopian solution to the Great War was a general armistice based on "Peace without victory," which Chesteron called war without excuse. Clemenceau, not a stranger to irony, said that Wilson's proposal was "What human beings might be capable of accomplishing if only they were not human." He would not have said that of Lincoln. For all its homespun idioms and melancholy, Lincoln's sense of humor was closer to the old English Whigs than the New England abolitionists or Wilsonian democrats. Coincidences would have been drolleries for Lincoln, and indiscretions for Wilson.

We Americans place such an exaggerated confidence in the power of politics to change things that we tend to interpret most acts politically, and this is the recipe for undisciplined moral zeal. Even philosophers and theologians are categorized as "conservative" or "liberal" and speech is either politically correct or incorrect. This was carried to an extreme when an American diplomat at the United Nations in the Clinton administration referred to Nelson Mandela as an "African American South African." No American in the audience seemed to think this linguistics odd, presumably because absurdity is not recognized as such by those who take politicized language seriously. Or when the Mayor of the City of New York announced that there are twenty-four million rats in his jurisdiction, no journalist questioned his statistic; and this was because civic righteousness was enlisted so earnestly in the cause of extermination that it would have been considered bad citizenship to ask how he knew there were twenty-four million, a suspiciously round figure, and not less or more. Had the Lord Mayor of London made such an announcement, it probably would have occasioned some quiet glee, especially among the rat catchers.

There may be fanatics who think coincidentalism is an eccentric hobby. Eccentricity is disdained among Americans as vigorously as enthusiasm is scorned by the English. This may partly be due to the insular English stress on individualism as a defining national virtue while intensity of feeling is an American posture. John of Gaunt's land was a "fortress built by Nature for herself"; John Winthrop's was "a city upon a hill." The Magna Carta was a blunt contract; the Declaration of Independence is enshrined in its own civic temple. An Englishman's home is his castle; an American dreams of building a castle. These are generalizations, but generalizations are an express train to the truth, and one we hope does not derail. I have indulged a natural instinct of curiosity about different cultures and clans, trusting that the more they are studied, the clearer will be their achievements and failures, their personalities and conditions; their inconsequence will be even more poignant when I have no point to make, no argument to pursue, and no theses to sustain.

Any consideration of coincidence requires a sense of humor, to which I have alluded, to prevent mental strain. So I should make a few remarks about the nature of humor in this context. It is a rare gift, and Hippolyte Taine said the very word "humor" was untranslatable into French. Given what I have said about national characteristics, we may appreciate why English humor is based on understatement. As understatement is a form of irony, it relishes the absurd. It revels in calculated absurdity, like Lewis Carroll and more sharply in the case of Jonathan Swift, who incarnated irony by being an Anglo-Irishman. An elegant exemplar in the twentieth century was P.G. Wodehouse, whose gift for self-parody may dazzle and distract his readers from his cogency. There is a whole social science in such lines as this: "It is not difficult to tell the difference between a Scotsman with a grievance and a ray of sunshine." I betray what may be a fixed point of view when I observe that if it is possible for one statement to be truer than another true statement, Wodehouse's remark might have been truer had he said "a Welshman." Other people interpret understatement as sullenness, which it is not. The confusion goes back a long way. A famous aphorism of the ancient Romans said that the English are a people typically given to crying and rarely to laughter: *Anglia gens est optima flens et pessima ridens*. But this only betrays the Latin tendency to laugh at what is not humorous, a characteristic which continues to the present day in southern Europe. It may be that the depressed behavior of the English was caused by the effect the Romans were having on them. The Romans did not understand that the English were laughing inside, and perhaps their insides were laughing inside, and perhaps their insides were laughing very much at the Romans.

The Oxford logician Richard Whately (who coincidentally died in the year of the Gettysburg Address) made a point at which the vulgar still laugh. He said that happiness is no laughing matter. But I suspect he was laughing to himself as he was making a most logical point about true joy. Some of the following chapters refer *en passant* to Alexander Pope and Jonathan Swift. Pope grandly boasted that he had never laughed in his life, and this I can believe because he hardly seemed a man of much humor. It is a different matter when Swift could remember having laughed only twice in his entire life. Frank Muir cites this with palpable pride in *The Oxford Book of Humorous Prose*. Swift was a very humorous man but not about the sort of thing one would laugh at. His epitaph pays tribute to his "savage indignation." If he had been French or German, that indignation would have reached high and dramatic pitch. As Swift was what he was, he channeled it into advice on the protocols of Lilliput and eating babies. When confronted with a blatant coincidence, the English tend to festoon it with wry condescension, while any number of Americans would invest it with solemn significance. To wallow in generalizations, let us say that other people would gingerly back away and drop the subject. But Swift's satire was a sincere bit of acting. There is a tendency among Americans to suspect that acting is insincere, which is why they would prefer that their actors be celebrities rather than be able to act. The more ironic English assume that any form of sincerity is bad acting, and so their celebrities must be actors. It is according to an unwritten constitution, and the monarchy itself, to be sincerely constitutional, must be a very high and noble act. Their Established Church is entirely an act, created by an act, and sustained by acts, and imperils itself when it dabbles in religion.

Against this background, the highest kind of humor is self-deprecating. As an after-dinner speaker, I once was introduced during dessert as a master of self-defecating humor. This alarmed some who were still alert, but I understood what the nervous chairman meant to say and I felt unworthy of the intended compliment. The ability to laugh at one's self is the perception of imbalance raised to a high moral level. Without self-deprecation, righteousness decays into self-righteousness and people given to it may flog themselves, but the effort defeats its purpose unless they can laugh at themselves while doing it, and this they will not do.

The following chapters were written first as magazine articles, and their literary quality is perforce limited and almost telegraphed in style. A tactless editor in his disregard for early Saxon kings and Hindu dynasties cut out whole bits here and there with the coldness of the Huns pillaging Aquileia. Then I was surprised that some readers reacted to the columns like the dog mentioned above. I was trying to point out the improbability of some coincidences, and they complained that the absurdity was absurd. They had difficulty following my train of thought, but this was because, as I have said, it was an express train. Of a more virulent pathology was that small group who thought that I made sense, blithely following what they thought was my logic to destinations unintended by me but agreeable to them.

One cannot regret them without expressing gratitude to those who offered helpful comments. A lawyer sent an article on the hydrogen sulfide content in cabbages, which he had found in a magazine published by Aer Lingus. In connection with the same item, a retired colonel sent me helpful information on the botany of cabbages to the study of which he has dedicated his golden years. A Franciscan friar pointed out that William Shakespeare and Shirley Temple have the same birthday. Then a Cardinal whose detailed knowledge of Rome is based on many years of living there told me that I had confused the Church of Santa Maria in trivia with Santi Vincenzo e Anastasio. I had no right to plead the ignorance of a stranger since I had lived 'round the corner of both for several years. The former, which was built by Cardinal Mazarin, is mentioned as the church in question by the inimitable Augustus Hare in *Walks in Rome*. It turns out, however, that Hare and I were wrong and His Eminence was right, and I have corrected the reference in this book.

I am no less grateful to those who offered unhelpful advice, for that kind of information was even more useful to my purposes. After writing about coincidences involving the name George, a correspondent sent belated information about George Caron who was the tail-gunner of the *Enola Gay*, the boxer Georges Carpentier who lost to Jack Dempsey in 1921,

George Westinghouse, George Papadopolous of Greece, George M. Cohan, and George Ruth who was more frequently called "Babe." When I had written about some coincidences involving brothers, one reader let me know that I had ignored the sons of Clovis: Charibert, Sigebert, and Chilperic. The last was a tragic figure, having failed to get four letters of his own invention added to the Latin alphabet. Then he got stabbed in the Forest of Chelles near Paris in 584. The acid insinuation from some correspondents was that I deliberately neglected such figures. When your frame of reference is everything, you will be pilloried for omitting anything. I plead that I cannot describe the whole world in the miniscule space of a magazine page.

After reading only a few columns, one reader complained that I was wasting my life, and I took his counsel to heart, although it was not original. The one truly rattling comment was more than criticism; it was like a ragged bolt of lightning. It came from a man in a town of Montana who accused me of anachronism in my dating of the Princess Elisa's accession to the Duchy of Lucca. He went to the length of saying that I was "cultivating weeds" by spreading false information.

It is not my intention to start a philosophical debate about coincidence. Carl Jung brought to the discussion what he supposed was a scientific element when he prescinded from the traditional meanings of synchronism to speak of "synchronicity" as an "acausal connecting principle." He thought that preoccupation with it could be hurtful to mental stability. I am in no position to evaluate that esoteric argument, though I think it touches the fringe of Gnostic superstition. There is a finer line between coincidence as providence and coincidence as chance, and this is left to theologians and their science, which is the highest of them all. I should not degrade what they have written on the subject by cursory allusions. The author of *Parallel Lives*, Plutarch, was fascinated with similar events in the lives of famous men. In the particular instance of Quintus Sertorius, the Roman statesman and general assassinated in 72 B.C., he suggested a sensible and natural explanation: coincidences are inevitable because circumstances are either so vast or so limited. "If the multitude of elements is unlimited, fortune has, in the abundance of her material, an ample provider of coincidences; and if, on the other hand, there is a limited number of elements from which events are interwoven, the same things must happen many times, being brought to pass by the same exigencies."

Odious as superstitious misuse of coincidences always is, only slightly less offensive is the underestimation of the significance of some of them. I mean the kind of coincidence which may not be only happenstance but which may be what has been called God's shorthand for a miracle, or God's way of remaining invisible. Some alignments of events are too portentous in their issue for the rational observer to treat as nothing more than oddities. I was in Rome in 1981 when the Pope was shot, and I stood on the spot where it had happened until late in the evening, thinking of how extraordinary it was that the day was May 13, the Feast of Our Lady of Fatima which is so closely intertwined with the drama of Marxism and dark predictions of suffering for the Church. I cannot speak for the Pope, much as I often volunteer to, but he offered thanks for his recovery by going to Fatima and presenting the bullet to the statue of the Blessed Virgin, so it is reasonable to infer that he saw more than quirk of timing in what happened. I was also at the World Trade Center on the fatal day in 2001. On another September 11, in 1683, King John Sobieski III assembled allied troops on the heights of Kahlenberg for the liberation of Vienna from the Ottoman army of Kara Mustafa, and on September 11 in 1697 Prince Eugene of Savoy dealt the final blow to the Ottoman army on the Serbian border at Zenta. This begs the question: was this an inexplicable web of events or was this data a conscious reference for men with terrible stratagems?

There are some coincidences, and their number may be as numberless as the stars, which oracles have called providential. If you are all tied up in yourself and think with the Atomists like Democritus that creation is an accidental interplay of atoms, providence is out of the question. Plato did not rule out providence, because he believed there is a hierarchy of gods arranging things: the supreme god who is involved in spiritual beings and general or universal entities such as classes and species and causes, the lesser gods who affect individual objects, and the demons who meddle in human affairs. So in our case, if we are classical Platonists, coincidences at best are rather suspicious caprices of evil powers. Aristotle imagined a more superior and singular deity, but that aristocratic god was contemplative thought, and it would be beneath the dignity of such a god to arrange coincidence.

The Lord of the Jews is far more splendid and grand in a gritty and palpable way, and he is also the subject of authentic revelation, truer than any force or entity the Greeks described, and his involvement in human affairs does not contradict history, because he created and sustains it. For the Jews, the one and only God governs events. The Sadducees, at least according to the historian Josephus, thought that direct divine in-

volvement with the human race would compromise moral freedom, so they said it could not be. A general affinity among the
Jews at the time of Christ seems to have been for inspired compromise on the subject: God does not force the human will, but
he does regulate circumstances as he divinely wills, and this in-
cludes the course of politics and society. When Christians declared that God had actually come into history as God and
man, the question was not whether God gets involved in making things happen, but rather to what extent he does it. If God
foresees actions and events, how can we ourselves be free
agents? It is a problem only for us who are confined to time and
space. Eternity is different and the eternal God can contemplate all that will be without compromising our moral freedom.
The First Vatican Council rejected theories of predestination
when it said that the free actions of creatures are not in any
way reduced by divine omniscience. The Council cited He-
brews 4:13: "For all things are naked and open to His eyes",
while reaffirming that everyone is accountable for his actions.
It is a bold assertion today when behaviorism has brainwashed
much of a whole generation into doubting the extent of moral
accountability.

Various economies of coincidence and fate are descants on a
basic affirmation in the sixth century by youthful Boethius, for
whom divine intelligence is superior to all things and directs all
things. As providence directs all things, St. Thomas Aquinas
understood it in terms of the virtue of prudence which cooper-
ates with God in ordering things toward their proper goal. So
the virtue of prudence is needed in analyzing whether a coincidence is more than a "mere" coincidence, and it is conspicu-
ously absent in those superstitious and fanatical people I

mentioned at the start, who get coincidence wrong. It is, for instance, the very opposite of prudence to submit to horoscopes, even though the Farnese pope, Paul III, relied on them to plan the minutest details of his daily schedule. The esoteric scheme of astrology assumes sympathetic causality, or the determining influence of dates and harmonies in the celestial spheres. As this cramps free will, it denies the action of grace, and so from a classical Christian point of view it is an affront to faith. A neurotic stock broker could become upset by the specter of fifty-five, for in 1929 and 1987 the New York Stock Exchange crashed fifty-five days after the market peaked. What would happen if speculators divested portfolios fifty-four days after each new height in the Dow Jones average? But as one of the inexplicable facts of history would have it, fifty-five was one of the seminal numbers in the *Liber Abaci* of the thirteenth-century mathematician Leonardo Fibonacci when he introduced to Latin culture the intricacies of Arabian and Indian number systems. As Leonard was often called Leonard Pisano, the hasty reader might confuse him with Antonio Pisano ("Il Pisanello"), the Veronese medalist. Leonardo would not have been surprised that Antonio died in the fifty-fifth year of the fifteenth century.

There are any number of shadings for synchronic phenomena: isochronism, consilience, syntony, concordance, concomilence, concurrence, and coetaneousness. As I have indicated, only delicate analysis can prudently measure whether we are reading too much into them or ignoring some higher intention which they express. Cardinal Newman posed the problem with typical elegance in the first volume of his *Essays Critical and Historical* with reference to the life of St. Ignatius: "The only further question which can be asked is, whether our argument does not prove too much . . . and therefore whether it is a mere coincidence ingeniously brought to light, and a gratuitous gloss on its meaning?" This is clear: coincidences cannot be chains which bind body and soul to some fatal governor. Should they sometimes evidence a divine pattern of will, the test is not how one succumbs to them but rather how one responds to them. A coincidence provided by God as a supernatural indication would be a moral challenge. The human will is free: "The evil perish not because they could not be good but because they did not want to be good..." The Council of Valence pronounced that in January 855, but there is no evidence of any significance in the fact that Vice President Schuyler Colfax was buried on the one thousandth anniversary of that day, having died in Mankato, Minnesota.

An evil generation seeks signs and wonders, and I am not the first to say it. But a stupid generation ignores signs and wonders. Whether or not synchronicity is a science (and I think it is not because science calculates according to observable patterns, and there is no predictability in coincidences, which is why we remark them), something can be read into any coincidence. The question is whether anything can be read out of it. When it comes to linking coincidence with providence, I remain on the whole prudently agnostic. Now I know painfully well that Lenin called agnosticism a fig leaf for materialism. I am not agnostic about God. I am agnostic about whether certain coincidental events bear the prints of God. Those who take a tabloid approach to the Scriptures and other venerable texts, use the synchronicity in them as a template for their own idiosyncrasies. They are tempted to detect messages encoded in the sacred texts. They may not be completely mistaken. A particular alignment of dates or numbers or events or personalities may or may not be "more" than coincidental, but in either case we can be edified that the question is raised. After all, the only reason for asking if a coincidence of things has a purpose is the belief that there is a purpose behind things. It is not a question for the Atomist. It is a plausible question for everyone else. The problem is, does a postmodern cultural analysis have the logical equipment to avoid both superstition and skepticism?

I have gone off on philosophical and theological paths when I only wanted to bask in the intertwining of explorers and engineers and singers and soldiers and poets. We should not begin a new millennium ignorant of an old one. Certainly it is not right that with so many ancestors we should rise up from the cradle of civilization as orphans. Indifference to past coincidences makes one a castaway in the journey of life, a tenant of oblivion, and a thrall to ennui much to be pitied.

We are not, however, interested in history as though it were only an entertainment, for more than one observer of the human comedy has warned that amusement can become the happiness of people who do not think. Herod Antipas was like that, and he received only silence from the Lord of History. Thought reveals the human tragedy in the human comedy. When Enoch Powell died in 1998, Charles Moore wrote in *The Daily Telegraph*: "Apprehension of the past made Powell's understanding of political events exceptionally deep and exceptionally painful. He suffered among his political contemporaries as a man with perfect pitch suffers among the tone-deaf." Lack of such apprehension leads to the "happy talk" that commentators chirp on television. That banality can transmogrify into a thing darker and destructive. I mean what is called "political correctness." The chilling Orwellian sound of it signals its viciously selfish plundering of reality. Great people change the course of history while demagogues change the facts of history. The latter find their prey among the witless that never were taught the facts.

I have used a somewhat arbitrary rule for giving dates in these chapters. It seemed pointless and patronizing to list dates that are common knowledge, like the Fourth of July or the Invasion of Gwalior. I have often given dates when I thought the reader might not have them at his immediate disposal or when they figured, say, numerically as the stuff of coincidence in themselves. Here then are the fifty essays, and I shall not pretend that the number is coincidental. It was a coincidence when I finished with forty-eight, because that was also the number of states in the Union before Alaska and Hawaii were admitted. It was even a coincidence when an extra chapter came to mind, for the arithmetic sum of four and nine is the number which more than any other has driven people to madness and hope.

Compulsive as I am about evenness and eager as I am for balance in the affairs of men and nations, I deliberately rounded the number of chapters to fifty. That is calculation and no coincidence at all: planning a coincidence is like planning an accident. But fifty is not an altogether innocuous number. Fifty was also the age of Mithradates VI Eupator when he fought the Roman invaders of Pontus, and of the Frenchman-turned-German romantic author Adelbert von Chamisso when he wrote *Frauenliebe und leben* which was set to music by Robert Schumann who moved to Dusseldorf in the fiftieth year of the nineteenth century. In 50 A.D. the Romans founded their colony at Colchester, and fifty years separated the Peace of Carlowitz from the Neapolitan reforms of Charles III. The Second Peloponnesian War began on the fiftieth birthday of Socrates, Agesilaus returned to Sparta on the fiftieth birthday of Aristophanes, and Callicrates became general of the Achaean League fifty years before the Roman conquest of Illyria. In our own day, the Crown Prince of Spain stood on the gaseous sands of Cape Canaveral watching a septuagenarian Senator John Glenn rise into space fifty years after the fiftieth anniversary of the Spanish-American War. An irresponsible mind may make too much of all these, but if the bare mention of them stimulates the mental appetite, the items which follow may be of interest. For reference purposes, it has not been possible to provide a complete guide to items cited in the text, so the reader is urged to follow the advice which appeared in the Sears and Roebuck catalogue of 1897: "If you do not find it in the index, look carefully through the entire catalogue."

THE ROMANCE OF WALES

EVELYN WAUGH DID NOT APPROVE OF READING ANY
book before reviewing it, or so he claimed in one of his curmud-
geonly posturings. His point, as I recall, was that to do so might
prejudice him. I have just come across a review by a critic who,
unlike Waugh, had thoroughly read the book in question and
liked it a lot, but feared that its voluminous references demanded
of the reader what he called a "world class" education. He
pointed out that beneficiaries of such pedagogy, among whom he
was quick to include himself, practically have disappeared. He
was right about that, but I do not want to address why this has
happened because the subject is too deep and there is nothing
like a lack of depth if you want clarity. One thing I should consider, though, and it should concern anyone with a sense of re-
sponsibility for shaping a generation to lead civilization into the
third millennium and it is this: the typical curriculum now de-
prives the student of the joy of genuine trivia. I do not mean
pedantry and computer nerdishness, but solemn high irrelevan-
cies. Some of the grimmest crimes against culture in modern

times have been the result of striving for relevance. Without information of irrelevance, the imagination will never experience the thrill of those curiosities which throughout the course of history have been the tonic of sober men, and the elixir of those less sober.

There are few finer ways to sharpen that imaginative faculty than to explore the strange interworkings and parallels by which the threads of human events have been worked in the woof and warp of history to produce the fantastic tapestry of coincidence. One predictable risk in a venture so vast is that from time to time this may actually slip into significance. Lord Byron hinted at that in *Don Juan*: "A 'strange coincidence', to use a phrase / By which such things are settled now-a-days." I can best explain this by producing some examples. For the sake of a theme here, to show how my system works, I shall take Wales, for I am writing on the bicentenary of the death of the mathematician, William Wales whose surname matched that principality and whose first name was the same as the pluralized surname of the Welsh composer, Thomas Williams, who was born at Ynysmeudwy in the Swansea Valley of Glamorganshire on the centenary of Mr. Wales's observation of the transit of Venus.

Let us begin at some remove. Even though our national system of education has collapsed, any high school student knows that in 1719 Prince Augustus of Saxony married a dwarf. Or at least, Archduchess Maria Josepha was so short that she was thought to be one. St. John Neumann was so short that he was chosen to hold the book up to the eye level of Pius IX as the Pope defined the dogma of the Immaculate Conception. He was the same height as St. Ignatius Loyola and St. John Vianney and James Madison (who also weighed exactly one hundred pounds). Little more than five feet tall, these men were still about four inches taller than St. Joan of Arc and Queen Victoria. But getting back to Augustus and Maria Josepha, the point I want to make is that their marriage, which was to be so sadly shadowed by the Silesian Wars, took place as the Welsh smelting industry was launched in Swansea.

Speaking of Wales, which most busy people rarely do, it is an interesting coincidence that the Prince of Wales was not the first brave heart to have wed a Lady Diana Spencer. In 1768 Lady Diana Spencer was married to Topham Beauclerk, Dr. Johnson's friend and a member of a large association as an illegitimate descendant of King Charles II. Beauclerk, eventually duke of St. Albans, was born to Nell Gwynn in the year that William Wales prepared to sail on Captain Cook's second voyage. Lady Diana and William Wales had the same birth year and she provided the illustrations for Dryden's *Fables*, which appeared in the year of Mr. Wales's death. And while the world knows that Henry Morton Stanley, a Welshman, found David Livingston, a Scot, at Ujiji in Central Africa in 1871, few are aware that Stanley also retrieved Edward Schnitzer, the German whom we usually speak of today as Emin Pasha, at Kavalli in 1888. Having claimed Tabora for Germany, the same Schnitzer was killed by Arabs in 1892, ironically near a waterfall named for Stanley.

So Wales, a land noble if not innocent of lethargy, is a blessed cornucopia of coincidence. The Prince of Wales's uncle, Lord Snowden (a title homophonic with the highest point in Wales), refined a lens for portrait photography and also designed the Penguin House at the London Zoo. The coincidence here lies with his sister, the Countess of Rosse in Ireland, a collateral descendant of the man who perfected the speculum of the reflecting telescope and whose fourth son designed snow chains used for automobile tires, which were used on one of the first expeditions to photograph penguins in Antarctica, almost literally poles apart from Captain Cook's third voyage to the Bering Strait, on which he once again was accompanied by the peripatetic Mr. Wales.

I make no apology for going off on a Welsh tangent. The romance of that land has its limits, but it should serve to remind us of those facts far stranger than fiction, knowledge of which is fast disappearing from our schools, and the study of which can raise us above the mire of the merely banal to the shimmering heights of the baroquely arcane.

LOVE FOR MINNEHAHA

IT IS CLUMSY TO SPEAK OF THE AMERICAN INDIAN AS A cipher for one people, for he was a cacophony of tribes and tongues; if you imagine him like a Remington silhouette scanning a reddened Midwestern prairie in the sunset, you might just as well think of him painting a psychedelic totem in the subarctic.

Years ago it was sociologically fashionable to refer to "Amerinds." That seems to have been replaced with "Native Americans" but everyone born today in Brooklyn has as much claim on that description. The diversity of the Indian was united by cords of dignity and hardships. His sufferings which were afflictions of nature elicit modern sympathy, and those which were inflicted by the white man elicit modern guilt. From the highest vaults of apophasis, I say that I will not mention the frequent cruelties of tribe to tribe, and of tribes to missionaries, or their screaming superstitions and inferior cosmology and very bad recipes. The same might be said, in one degree or another, of every culture that ever was, with the

single exception of France under Charles X.

Though not an Indian myself, it was my privilege in fact to attend an academy for Indians in New England. We had a school song, one of the finest ever written, about the first student, the Sachem of the Wah-Hoo-Wahs whose whole curriculum, in a happily rhymed couplet, was five hundred gallons of New England rum. I must admit that it pales, as it were, when compared with "Hiawatha's Wooing" by the Native-American poet Longfellow:

> "From the waterfall he named her,
> Minnehaha, Laughing Water."

Minnehaha was all lovely as the woods in the moonlight, and though Longfellow may have overlooked her smallpox, she was truer than the Walt Disney Corporation's vulgarization of the Anglican Pocahontas as a shill for the Green Party.

Each Thanksgiving season, reverie turns to that excellent man of the Pawtuxet tribe, Squanto, who died two years after the arrival of the metaphysical cranks known as the Pilgrim Fathers. For years before these radicalized Separatists arrived in Plymouth Bay, the Portuguese were fishing the rich coastal areas of Maine. It seems quite likely that Squanto was abducted, or enlisted, by them and taken back to Portugal, and then made his way to England. There he joined up with some fishermen who also had an active trawling industry in northern New England waters. Having lived with them long enough to learn some of their language, he sailed with them to the Maine fisheries, eventually working his way south to his native tribal area. After the *Mayflower* deposited her sober jetsam on Plymouth Rock, Squanto happened to be right there astonishing the passengers by greeting them in a heavy Bristol accent: "Welcome, Englishmen." Any normal shipload of tourists on a Cunarder would have called this an amusing coincidence, but the Puritans lapsed into Psalms, in the belief that this was the fulfillment of the Book of Daniel. Squanto helped the Pilgrim Fathers survive their first winter, and thus the American Indian and the Portuguese are indirectly responsible for three hundred years of neurotic New England Yankees.

This incident would have a sequel in 1808 when the Osage tribe ceded its lands to the government of the United States, for in that year the Yankee sealing captain Mayhew Folger happened upon Pitcairn Island and found English-speaking inhabitants who knew the word "ship" but had never seen one. They were children of crewmen of the *Bounty* who had mutinied in the same year as the French Revolution, just months after their leader Fletcher Christian had his buttocks tattooed on Tahiti in the Polynesian fashion.

The noble American Indian had the hapless duty of teaching the Puritans how to party. The coastal tribes of the American northeast equated feasting with a gargantuan abuse of food and drink. Among them, as among the post–Augustan Romans, celebratory dining had become virtually synonymous with regurgitating. The gathering place along the Schuylkill

River in Pennsylvania, still known as Manayunk, and the gathering place in New York still known as Manhattan, take their names from "meneiunk" and "manna ha ta" which mean "place where we go to drink." The New York Chamber of Commerce contests the almost certain evidence that "manna ha ta" was an intensifier whose more precise meaning is, "place where we go to vomit."

Another coincidence in the Indian saga centers on the date of September 15, 1830, when the Choctaw Indians ceded their lands east of the Mississippi to the United States, in the Treaty of Dancing Rabbit Creek. On the same day, history's first railway fatality occurred during the ceremonious dedication of the Liverpool and Manchester Line. William Huskinsson was run over by a steam engine as he reached out to shake the hand of the Duke of Wellington some seventeen miles outside Liverpool. Huskinsson was a very important leader of the House of Commons and a native Englishman. Wellington was a native Irishman, although he claimed to be English since, as he sensibly but insensitively put it, being born in a stable does not make a man a horse. In those fell and fatal hours of 1830, the age of the long-distance passenger railway had arrived, and the buffalo was wandering into the ghost lands.

Cast a cold eye on those centuries and the Indian pageant looks like some anthropological curiosity fit for a few display cases in the Museum of Natural History. But the wise heart senses more. As drums beat in mossy forests, a strange fellowship gazes from the campfires: not Minnehaha who never was though we love her anyway, but Portuguese sailors, Squanto, flinty Puritans, and the depressed Mr. Huskinsson.

SUCH GREAT NAMES AS THESE

A COMMERCIAL BANK NEAR ME HAS BEEN REDECORATED to celebrate the change of its name. Several indifferent but well-done oil portraits of Edwardian trustees have been replaced with poor prints of impressionist clichés covered with Plexiglass and rock music has been piped in. This grand Temple of Mammon has suffered its own liturgical movement.

Changes like that may not eliminate what is, but they do indicate what people in charge want a fact to become. Biblical figures are the same people after their names are changed, but the alteration signifies a new vocation or status. It was true of Abram turned Abraham all the way to Simon made Cephas. The effect is freighted with meaning theologically, historically, and psychologically.

Less appreciated is the amiable science of names that do not change but coincide. Marvelous can be the symmetry between one name and another, or between names and events. A book could not contain a small fraction of them, and the most famous hardly bear repeating: like Lincoln having had a secretary

named Kennedy when he was shot, and Kennedy having had a secretary named Lincoln when he was shot. As for rude and vulgar coincidences in names, all should yield to the advice of the Apostle Saul-Paul: "nec nominetur in vobis." But those with mental equipment prepared for wonder should consider just a few specimens.

The Corsican revolutionary, Pasquale di Paoli (1725–1807) was a contemporary of the Bavarian composer Christoph Willibald Gluck (1714–1787) and Gluck was a revolutionary of sorts himself, in his influence on opera. But many may have forgotten, or perhaps never knew, that another of the Glucks, the Austrian author Barbara Gluck (1814–1894), wrote under the pen-name Betty Paoli. Speaking of writers, it seems very curious that two who were distinguished for their imagination should have had singularly redundant names: Jerome Klapka Jerome (1859–1927) and Ford Madox Ford (1873–1939). Actually, Ford's real name was Hueffer, and Ford Madox Ford does not sound half as strange as Hueffer Madox Hueffer. The humorist Jerome (I refer to his surname as I would not presume to address him by his Christian name) was born in the year of the death of Josip-Jelacic of Buzima, that remarkably unhumorous governor of Croatia and Slovenia.

Literary trivia attains to grandeur in the instance of the twentieth century's greatest man. For Winston Churchill (1874–1965) was a contemporary of the American writer Winston Churchill (1871–1947). Both attended service academies: Sandhurst and Annapolis. The American Winston published his novel *Coniston* in the same year, 1906, that English Winston published *Lord Randolph Churchill*. It is as confusing as the two Eulalias martyred under Diocletian in 304; they can only be distinguished by the one coming from Barcelona and the other from Merida.

Only on Judgment Day may we know the significance of Thackeray's eponymous Barry Lyndon being the name of the Australian mayor responsible for so much of Melbourne's neoclassical architecture. Then, too, may we divine the strange workings by which the English actor and playwright, Samuel Foote (1720–1777), suffered the amputation of a foot in 1766. At least their names are easier to pronounce than Shchedrin, the pen name of Mikhail Evgrafovich Saltykov (1826–1889), which the French in one of their little ways pronounce

Chtchedrine. Shchedrin wrote the *Satires in Prose* in the year Thackeray died.

In the classical realm: the first ruler of Rome was Romulus, the first emperor of Rome was Augustus (Octavianus), and the last Roman emperor was Romulus Augustus. And on the Byzantine side, the first and last emperors of Constantinople were named Constantine (the last being Constantine XI Palaeologus). The name Hamilcar, now rare even in the suburbs, belonged to both the fifth century (B.C.) Carthaginian general who marched on Sicily, and the third century (B.C.) general in Sicily (whose son, of course, was Hannibal).

Regarding place names, the capitals of St. Petersburg in Russia and Williamsburg in Virginia were founded and given Dutch names within a few years of each other. Czar Peter, you see, was fond of things Dutch, and King William of England (and Virginia) was of the Dutch House of Orange. William of Orange brings to mind the energumenous Oliver Cromwell (1599–1658). That name should ring a special bell for Americans, because Mr. Justice Holmes (1841–1935) became Chief Justice of Massachusetts on the centenary of the resignation of Mr. Justice Ellsworth (1745–1807) as Chief Justice of the Supreme Court of the United States, which was also the tercentenary of the birth of Oliver Cromwell. And to top that, both Holmes and Ellsworth were named Oliver. Ellsworth, by the way, died on the two thousandth anniversary of Hannibal's victory over the Carthaginian troops in a bloody confrontation at the Metaurus River. His brother Hasdrubal died in that engagement taking to his grave the same name as the cavalry commander who fought so bravely for Hannibal at Cannae. Another Ellsworth, with Lincoln for his first name, an explorer funded by the Johns Hopkins University, published *The Last Wild Buffalo Hunt* on the two thousandth anniversary of Hannibal's departure from Capua with all his elephants.

Diomed, or Diomedes for the purists, is a splendid name, recalling the legendary King of Argos who helped Odysseus steal the statue of Pallas Athena, known as the Palladium. When the hippophilic Duke of Wellington was simply Colonel Arthur Wellesley (1769–1852), he named his horse Diomede. On the fiftieth anniversary of the Iron Duke's death, Archbishop Falconio resigned his post as Apostolic Delegate to Canada, evidently unaware that his baptismal name—guess what it was—gave him something in common with the Duke's noble steed.

LEARNING
GEOGRAPHY

THE REVEREND SAMUEL WESLEY (1662–1735) LIVED IN
an age which is commonly caricatured as one of beef and ale
and good cheer. But years after his rectory burned to the
ground, he wrote a lengthy *Dissertations on the Book of Job* and a
collection of poetry entitled *Maggots*. No one would have mistaken him for Dr. Norman Vincent Peale. Fifteenth among his
eighteen children, whom he fathered in hopes of domestic bliss,
was John. Now John picked up his father's insect motif when
his fellow precursors of Methodism were called "Bible Moths."
On the whole, he was cheerful in spite of his marriage to the
beclouded Mary Vazeille. No one would have mistaken her for
Mrs. Norman Vincent Peale.

One sober biographer attributes John's cheerfulness to emotional imbalance, but this is no explanation for the unrelieved
cheerfulness of the youngest Wesley, Charles. This pious
prodigy wrote slightly more than 6,100 hymns and finally quit
when his mind was exhausted, unlike some of our more persistent modern hymn writers. My only reason for mentioning all

this is: if each of Charles Wesley's hymns counted as a square mile, the sum would equal precisely the surface mass of the Chesapeake Bay. This little survey serves well to point up the similarity and greater dissimilarity between biography and geography. Chesterton's young classmate at St. Paul's School, Edmund Clerihew Bentley, put it precociously and unsurpassedly in what is now known as the "Clerihew" form of rhyme:

> The art of Biography
> Is different from Geography.
> Geography is about maps,
> But Biography is about chaps.

An alert eye will spot many such coincidences in geography sufficient unto themselves for interest, though they fascinate most when intertwined with biography. I found geography a dismal science in school, when it was just a matter of memorizing state capitals (often the most inappropriate cities) and boundaries (which are only logical in the square states). It became more complicated when a lot of places on various continents yielded to the meddlers and changed their names altogether. Fortunately, I have retained a small globe of our planet with the real names intact, like French Equatorial Africa and so forth. At most, there should be a dozen nations, with appendages all around. Were this column not limited, I could make a strong case for the happier condition of such a world. But to the point: geography would not be the horror it is to the psychologically healthy child if the creature were shown a science which vaults over bland latitudes and longitudes to the romance of the people who explored them.

For example, I have vivid recollections of the night of June 26, 1959 when Ingemar Johansson defeated Floyd Patterson for the heavyweight championship by a knockout in the third round. A golden opportunity was lost when geography teachers throughout the United States, including mine, failed to point out that it was the two hundredth anniversary of the death of the astronomer Pierre Louis Moreau de Maupertuis whom King Louis XV had sent to measure longitude in Lapland. He had Newton for a friend and Voltaire for an enemy, so he must have been a great man. I was the sort of student who discovered the connection between 1959 and 1759 on my own. From the perspective of New Jersey, where I was located at the time, Lapland was easily confused with Johansson's Sweden. But the coincidence satisfied me and, more importantly, was the type of thing that annoyed one's teacher when it was brought to her attention.

Ironically, Greenland was named by Eric the Red. Even more effervescent is the saga of the Congo River. While the most lethargic student knows that it was named for the Bacongo tribe, whose rituals would have darkened the gloom of the Rev. Mr. Samuel Wesley, I was surprised in Lisbon to hear the name of Diogo Cão, who discovered the river's mouth, pronounced akin to "Congo." Then there is the strangest fact about Honeyville, Utah, a euphonious contraction of Hunsakerville, the original name honoring its first settler: it was also the name of the Annapolis graduate and chief of aeronautical design for the Navy Department, Jerome Clarke Hunsaker, who designed the first airship to cross the Atlantic, the NC4.

I have never been invited to teach a class in geography. If I did, I would not begin with the dull formalities that are the affliction of such instruction. Were I called upon to open the lay of the land to young minds, I would begin with something riveting, say perhaps a description of the Meander River in Turkey. It has over a thousand bends. Then I would explain that its twisting shape has endowed the English vocabulary with the neo-Turkish verb "to meander." If you add one "n", you have Menander. And Menander, who flourished two centuries before Christ, was that amazing man of the Greco-Bactrian dynasty who meandered for years until he invaded India, conquered the valley of the Indus, the Punjab and Gujarat, and became a Buddhist. After just one such class, I am sure that I would have turned many a child into a geographer for life.

OF CABBAGES
AND KINGS

ALICE WAS PERPLEXED IN *Through the Looking Glass* WHEN
the Walrus said it was time to talk of many things:

> Of shoes—and ships—and sealing wax—
> Of cabbages—and kings—
> And why the sea is boiling hot—
> And whether pigs have wings.

On this side of the Looking Glass, not the Walrus but the
former Vice President of the United States has written a book
in which he seems to fear that the sea is indeed about to boil.
And animal rights activists have decided that pigs do have
wings, though only the pure in heart can see them. But few
people today talk about cabbages and kings. The silence about
cabbages is due to hypocrisy. Vegetarians reject the seamless
garment of culinary issues: they feel sorry for roast pigs
while subjecting cabbages to a thousand humiliations from
shredding to pickling, condemning frankfurters while relishing

sauerkraut, and never asking the olive how cold is it at the bottom of a martini. Unlike the case with cabbages, hesitancy about kings is due not to hypocrisy but to envy. Kings will always be victims of the Green-Eyed Monster so long as there can be on average no more than one king per country.

Perhaps the Walrus was on to something. The curtain rises on the stage of history to reveal uncanny coincidences involving cabbages and kings. Consider three different men whom we associate with heroic rescues: Pliny the Elder, Diocletian, and Gallieni. Pliny (23–79 A.D.) led a rescue mission when Mount Vesuvius erupted and died in the effort off the coast of Herculaneum. Troops of the emperor Gaius Aurelius Valerius Diocletian (245–312) rescued Constantius (c.250 –306) when he was besieged by more than 6,000 Alemanni at Langres. During the first Battle of the Marne in the First World War, the military governor of Paris, Joseph Simon Gallieni (1849–1916) mobilized a convoy of city taxicabs to transport 80,000 reserves to the beleaguered troops of Manoury's Sixth Army, repulsing General Alexander von Kluck and saving Paris. All three of these men played parts in the lore of the cabbage.

First, Pliny among many other things was a naturalist who identified six varieties of the cabbage in the *Historia Naturalis*. Second, Diocletian abdicated in 305 and spent his last years in Split in his native Dalmatia enjoying his favorite pastime, which was raising cabbages. Third, the troops of Gallieni rode in their taxicabs to the Marne singing songs about the "Boches", a derogatory term for Germans from *coboche* meaning "cabbage head" derived from the Latin *caput*, or "head", which both Pliny and Diocletian used as slang for cabbage. Diocletian's death brings to mind Juvenal's sage warning in the *Satires*: "Occidit miseros crambe repetita magistros" which basically means that overcooked cabbage can wear out the master's life.

I fear that in relating these things, I am belaboring the obvious. But not everyone remembers that Old King Cole of the nursery rhyme was the ancient British king, Coel of Caernarfon whose name is homophonic with "cole." This plant, from the Latin *caulis* is of the same species (Brassica) as the cabbage, and may have been the vegetable in the bowl for which the jolly old soul called Cole, or "colewort", is the source of cole slaw or, more precisely colewort slaw or, more fancifully, coelwort slaw. The typical man in the street probably persists in the belief that Coel of Caernarfon's daughter was St. Helena, the wife of Constantius and mother of Constantine. But Coel's real daughter was Helen, who married Magnus Clemens Maximus (fl.383–388), the emperor whom the emotional Welsh revere as the mythic hero Maxen Wledig. By him, Helen bore a son Custennin, the name being a variant of Constantine. Hence the widespread confusion.

The real St. Helena was the daughter of an innkeeper of Drepanum in Bithynia, which is why snobbish Diocletian, the cabbage king, ordered Constantius to divorce her. She was lovelier to behold than Constantius. His pallid complexion gained him the nickname *Chlorus*, a latinization of the Greek for pale green which is sometimes interpreted "cabbage-faced." St. Helena brought to Cologne what she thought were the relics of the Three Kings. Later, the Farina brothers of Cologne invented a scent which they called *Acqua Admirabilis*. After the Seven Years' War, it was exported to Britain as "Cologne water" and can be found today in the shops of Colchester, once known as Caernarfon, or Camulodunum to the Romans, the royal city of King Coel.

In 1996, on the sesquicentenary of the first commercial treaty between the United States and the Kingdom of Hanover (where, says Browning of Hamelin, "The river Weser, deep and wide / Washes its walls on the southern side"). Chancellor Helmut Kohl of Germany co-authored with his wife, Hannelore, a cookbook containing ten recipes for their namesake cabbage. So it is indeed, a very small world after all. And as Alice would have said in Wonderland, it becomes "Curiouser and curiouser!"

INTESTINAL
FORTITUDE

IN 782, CHARLEMAGNE SUPPRESSED A SAXON UPRISING led by the Westphalian chieftain Widukind, and massacred 4,500 captives in revenge for the annihilation of his own army three years earlier at Süntelberg. The fields were drenched in gore for days, and pagan Widukind quickly asked to be baptized at Attigny. No one gazing upon that melancholy landscape could have predicted that, on the millennium of the battle, the Montgolfier brothers would make their first successful launch of a heated air balloon. Unnoticed in that giddy year of 1782 were the births of the poet Esias Tegner, who might well be called the Swedish Kochanowski, and history's greatest violinist, Niccolo Paganini.

Paganini suffered from numerous intestinal complaints, and nearly died from an infection in 1823. In November, he wrote to a friend ironically named Germi: "I am almost a miracle. An American doctor has saved me . . . the cough will go, little by little." As that unnamed American was performing his skills, the Monroe Doctrine was being proclaimed back in his own

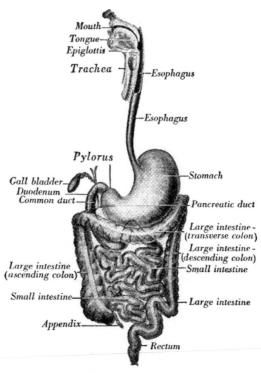

Fig. 450. *Digestive, or Alimentary, Canal
of Man* [1]

country, and Lord Byron was joining up with the insurgent Greeks.

At the behest of the future Princess Marie Anne Elisa of Lucca, Paganini had written his undying "Sonata for the G String" in 1799 naming it for her brother Napoleon, who had been appointed First Counsel with Cambaceres and Lebrun and by whose grace the proud father of the Montgolfier brothers would be granted a peerage. Most likely, Napoleon habitually kept his hand inside his waistcoat because of an ulcer although he seems to have given others more ulcers than he got himself. The "Sonata" which Paganini played on his favorite violin, a Guarnerius given him by a French merchant in Lugano, enjoyed a rapturous reception, but envious malcontents spread a rumor that the instrument's string was part of his wife's intestine. This distressed Paganini while increasing public interest in his recitals. Giuseppe Guarneri, by the way, belonged to a family of distinguished violinmakers in Cremona in the seventeenth and eighteenth centuries. There were in fact two craftsmen with the same name: one a son of the master Andrea, and another a nephew. One will not want to be confused by a magical coincidence: born in 1856 as Laura Keene was opening her musical theatre in New York and dying in 1918 at the same age as Andrea's nephew Giuseppe, the greatest of the Guarneris, was the pathologist Giuseppe Guarneri who invented a virtually foolproof method for diagnosing smallpox.

Paganini cast off this mortal coil on a balmy day in 1840. Seated in his villa in Nice, near a portrait of Byron (who had died in 1824 in Missolonghi from a fever after eating sausage), the prodigy adjusted the cat gut on his violin, and began to play ethereal improvisations. Suddenly the bow dropped and that romantically tortured figure was gathered up by his Muse to a height no heated air balloon can reach. It was the centenary of the birth of Joseph Michel Montgolfier, whose earliest research on inflatable apparatus had involved the use of cattle bladders. In exploit, he had been matched only by the expatriate Boston physician, John Jeffries, who stitched together a gaseous balloon with his fine surgical hands and crossed the English Channel by air on January 7, 1785. As Paganini lay finally free of earthly constraints, the embalmed corpse and viscera of Napoleon were interred in Paris after his long exile.

In the pageant of religion, it is believed that the over-wrought sentiments in Martin Luther's *Wider das Papsttum zu Rom* were the product of colonic impactions in 1545. More familiar is the morality tale of Louis XIV's late mistress, the Duchesse de La Vallière, whose intestines were accidentally dropped and eaten by pigs in 1710. Doubtless, the most famous painting of an intestine is Nicholas Poussin's *Martyrdom of Saint Erasmus*, now in the Pinacoteca of the Vatican, which has attracted gastroenterologists since its completion in 1629. The masterpiece was returned to Rome, Italy, through the diplomacy of Cardinal Consalvi in 1817, the same year that Governor DeWitt Clinton broke ground in Rome, New York, for the Erie Canal. Consalvi's advisor was Canova who had sculpted a bust of Paganini's patroness, the Princess Elisa.

Ever since the death of Sixtus V, pontifical entrails had normally been enshrined across from the Trevi Fountain in the Church of St. Vincenzo e Anastasio. But in 1846 the munificent Pius IX permitted the canons of Valence to keep the internal organs of Gregory XVI in their cathedral. Gregory XVI succeeded Pius VIII, the successor of Leo XII, who had made Paganini a Knight of the Golden Spur in 1827, the same year in which the English environmentalist, Peter Baume, stipulated in his last will and testament that his bones be made into knife handles and buttons, and his internal organs be used as fertilizer. This was carried out in 1829 and, as his upper and lower intestines were being planted in his favorite rose garden, Parliament passed the Catholic Relief Act.

In 1802, in his *Traité du physique et du moral de l'homme*, Pierre Cabanis, physician to Mirabeau and father of physiological psychology, claimed that all poetry and religion are products of the smaller intestines. Thomas Carlyle mocked him for this, and rightly so, for the conceit is far more cynical than Descartes' naive location of the soul in the pineal gland. But the inspired word (1 John 3:17) speaks of the "bowels of compassion", and I would avoid those modern versions that translate "bowels" as "heart." I would also avoid the translators.

SEEKING COMMON GROUND

AMONG TRUISMS, ONE OF THE MORE CONTESTABLE IS that opposites attract. What is true, say, of magnetic poles is not a universal in human relations. A fair woman may attract an ugly man; the ugly man does not necessarily therefore attract a fair woman. What is far more often true, is that opposites are similar. Otherwise, there would be little point in remarking their differences. Aristotle made a name for himself by pointing this out.

Take the case of the repellent Fuehrer. In studying the career of that angular personality, we cannot help but be struck by the difference between Adolf Hitler and Louisa May Alcott. *Mein Kampf* is antithetical in every way to *Little Women*. But both authors died at the age of fifty-six, and so did Abraham Lincoln. Yet, if Herr Hitler had given an address at Gettysburg, it would have been longer and different in tone; and Miss Alcott's Gettysburg Address would have been sympathetic, but not so lapidary. Oddly, too, Hitler and Queen Elizabeth II were born, in different years, but within the same twenty-four-hour cycle of April 20–21, providing a challenge for the horoscope people.

At the end of a play in which Sarah Bernhardt played the role of Cleopatra, Max Beerbohm overheard two matrons remarking how very unlike were the home lives of the Queen of Egypt and Queen Victoria. Both queens knew inconsolable grief, but Victoria never ran through the corridors of Windsor with an asp on her bosom. Two men might have remarked a similar contrast between Mark Antony and Prince Albert. The domestic arrangements of Antony in Alexandria were not those of Albert at Osborne House. And that is precisely my point: the difference is noteworthy only because of the similarity between monarchs, triumvirs, and consorts. Their congruity is the very spice of their incongruity.

I can illustrate this with two names which invariably will come up in any discussion of the social history of the twentieth century: Gertrude Ederle and King Ibn Saud. We instinctively link them because Miss Ederle at the age of nineteen became the first woman to swim the English Channel in the same year, 1926, that Saud became Sultan of the Nejd, completing the great athletic feat in 14 hours and 31 minutes. Yet the English Channel is as wet as the Nejd is arid. And Saud maintained notorious strictures, to the extent of maiming, against any woman wearing a bathing costume.

Why is the popular imagination still fascinated by the Merovingian hero and king of all the Franks, King Dagobert I? It may be because this illiterate, who believed that writing instruments are effete, allowed St. Amand to baptize his son Sigebert exactly twelve hundred years before John Joseph Parker invented the fountain pen in 1832. Parker, incidentally, was a

namesake of the commander of the Minutemen at the Battle of Lexington, which was fought on April 19, 1775, the eleven hundredth anniversary of the death of St. Amand.

While countless people have had bad gums, the reason we remember that the scientific King Charles III of Spain had periodontal disease is that he died in 1788 just as the French dental pioneer, Nicholas Dubois de Chemant, introduced an improved type of porcelain denture. As incongruous congruities go, that was morally indifferent. Not so the paradox of the German philologist Frederick August Wolf, who was the world's foremost expert on Helen of Troy. He died in 1824, the very year of the establishment of the Rensselaer School of Theoretical and Practical Science in, of all places, Troy in New York. Chiefly because of that coincidence is it interesting that the school's purpose of replacing the classical curriculum with studies in applied science and engineering contradicted every pedagogical principle Wolf held dear in his *Darstellung der Al-*

tertumswissenschaft. Wolf maintained in his *Prolegomena ad Homerum* that various authors had their hands in writing the *Iliad* and the *Odyssey*. This sensational work, which anticipated some of the nineteenth-century biblical form critics in Germany, was published in the year that Stephen Van Rensselaer, founder of the Troy school, became lieutenant governor of New York.

If the veil were rent in twain on the pantheon of contradictory coincidences, we would certainly encounter Miler McGrath, the Irish Franciscan who, for nine years during the reign of Elizabeth I, was simultaneously the Catholic and Protestant bishop of Cashel. His tomb at the "Rock of Cashel" is well worth a visit, particularly for the inscription which is lyrically critical of him. As he anticipated in malleability of virtue the Vicar of Bray, it is amusing that a far more principled successor from 1792 to 1820 was Archbishop Bray. McGrath may be the prototype of the hasty ecumenicist for whom unity is not an impossible Philosopher's Stone, provided one compromises essentials. People like him are not "signs of contradiction." They function rather as contradictions of contradictions, and their cynicism gushes like a hydrant from the waterpipes of pride. It is no coincidence at all that there should be so many like Miler McGrath who think that, by emphasizing similarities between things, they can make things the same.

A CORNUCOPIA OF
PHARMACOPOEIA

THE SCOTS ARE FAMOUSLY RESERVED IN THEIR HABITS
and modest in demeanor, but this has not restrained their substantial claim to be the world's most intelligent people. In the
catalogue of certifiable evidence is this curiosity: although the
Scots comprise less than one half of 1 percent of the world's
population, 11 percent of all the Nobel prizes have been
awarded to Scotsmen. The world's first university faculty of engineering and technical science was in Glasgow. Scotsmen
have shown particular genius in medicine, as we saw in the
cloning of sheep in the 1990s by Dr. Ian Wilmut, whose wife is
a Presbyterian elder.

Scotland, the home of famous preachers is also the home of
anesthesia. Samuel Guthrie, a Scottish-American, co-discov-
ered chloroform in 1831. Sir James Young Simpson first used it
in surgery in 1847 in Scotland, the year after the Scottish-
American, William Thomas Green Morton demonstrated the
use of ether as an anesthetic in Boston. Before any of them, in

1829, James Esdaile used hypnosis in surgery while in India, having been inspired by charmed cobras.

David Livingston, who secured the abolition of slavery in Zanzibar in 1873, was a physician, as was John Brown, who in 1780 had argued successfully against bloodletting. Charles Maitland beat William Jenner in using vaccinations, albeit leaving Scotland to experiment on eighty-five Londoners; and in 1913 William Leishman perfected the typhoid vaccine. It may be that more lives have been saved by Sir Patrick Manson, who traced parasitic diseases to biting insects, and Sir Alexander Fleming, who discovered penicillin in 1928, than by any other two men in history. If one rejects the influences of environment and race, one must attribute all this to coincidence.

Among problematic coincidences is the fact that almost all the pioneers in modern gynecology have been Scottish Presbyterians. The influence of Presbyterianism on gynecology has been subtle, perhaps their only connection is the Greek of their names. The Calvinism of Scotland advertised a lack of sympathy for women in 1558 when John Knox published his *First Blast of the Trumpet against the Monstrous Regiment of Women*, directed with no ambiguity against Mary of Guise. So it is not to be supposed that any single doctrine of Presbyterianism guided the Scottish penchant for gynecology.

It was a Scottish Presbyterian, William Smellie (1697–1753), who first involved professional physicians in midwifery. Dr. Smellie also researched the putrefaction of corpses, but he is known to medical history as the inventor of the "long obstetric forceps" used on Queen Charlotte by the Scottish founder of modern obstetrics, William Hunter (1718–1783), whose brother John (1728–1793) was the father of scientific surgery.

The ovum in mammals was discovered by William Cruickshank (1745–1800) and Matthew Bailey (1761–1823) invented treatment for dermoid cysts in the ovary. All of them were devout Scottish Presbyterians as was Alexander Skene (1837–1900) who emigrated from Aberdeen and founded the American Gynecological Society.

Ephraim McDowell (1771–1830) studied medicine at the University of Edinburgh, and practiced his art on the American frontier, performing the world's first ovariotomy on Jane Todd Crawford, a Scotswoman in Kentucky. The future President, Andrew Jackson, of Scottish line, once assisted Dr. McDowell in a surgical operation, remarking afterwards that he would rather fight another Indian war than repeat the experience. And another future President of Scottish blood, James Knox Polk, age seventeen, had a gallstone removed from his bladder by the indefatigable Dr. McDowell, proving that the goodly physician did not confine his healing arts to the fairer sex. Polk kept the stone as a souvenir and took it to the White House.

Other Celtic peoples have chiefly confined their medical inventiveness to homeopathy. Underlying the phenomenal link between Calvinist Celts and female medicine may have been an unconscious desire to correct the exaggerated sentiments of John Knox. Perhaps it has had something to do with the intercessions of Mary Queen of Scots who was the principle audience of Knox's blasts after the death of her mother, and whose husband, in a setback for Scottish medicine, was blown up. But even John Knox formerly had been a child, and had at least that in common with his theological opponents. Queen Victoria also passed through a period of infancy, and when affairs of nature and state conspired to oblige her to bear children, she was chloroformed by the aforementioned Scot, Dr. Simpson, whom she knighted.

Motherhood is the greatest ecumenical movement. And despite the propensities of Scotsmen for theological meanderings, the dogma of the Immaculate Conception has Scottish credentials; it was once scorned by some medieval scholastics as a "Scotist opinion" because it was identified with Duns Scotus born in Duns, Berwickshire. And the Jews, whose midwifery is even older than that of the Scots, may be doubly thanked for the Blessed Lady, and for the philanthropic patron of medical research, Sir Isaac Wolfson, son of a Scottish-Jewish mother.

NEITHER UP
NOR DOWN

IN 1996, THE SCHOOL BOARD OF OAKLAND, CALIFORNIA
caused a stir by trying to recognize a dialect of English as a separate language. According to the *New York Times*, this form
known by the neologism "Ebonics" has several characteristics,
which include the use of a pronoun instead of the infinitive "to
be", dropping standard conjugations, eliminating subject-verb
agreement, and replacing the qualifier "if" with the imperative
"do." The adventurous syntax produces such lines as: "My
friend he smarter than you. He have more brains. I ask him do
he knows the answer." There is much to this that I find beguiling, especially since I have long advocated the Tudor first person negative "ain't", which in fact enjoyed a minor revival in
country-house circles of the 1920s: pace Lord Peter Wimsey. It
can also be argued that what seems an abuse of certain infinitives actually has roots in the Elizabethan subjunctive. What I
do object to is the suggestion that all this is the brainchild of
the Oakland School Board. Thirty years ago, the International

Commission on English in the Liturgy invented a proleptical and prolegomenous form of "Ebonics" for the new vernacular Mass. Catholics in America have thus been speaking this way since Vatican II.

Mark Twain deftly mastered the syntax, as did the nineteenth-century repertoire of dialect songs, like those of Stephen Foster. One might protest that these were affectations of an idiom, but so were the many wistful Irish songs written by the agile Jewish song masters of Schubert Alley. The most distinguished precursor of ebonical syntax in drama, after Harriet Beecher Stowe, was Dion Boucicault, whose play *The Octoroon* opened in the Winter Garden in New York City on December 5, 1859. By a strange coincidence, that was the day Senator Charles Sumner returned to his Senate desk after having been beaten with a cane by Senator Preston S. Brooks on May 22, 1856 during a debate over slavery in Kansas. No such violence has yet been inflicted on a liturgical translator, not even on those responsible for the alternative opening collects of the ebonical *Novus Ordo*, the English translation of the *Roman Rite* which parses like Thomas Cranmer on Prozac.

Another fascinating association has been evoked by the controversy in recent decades over "gender inclusive" language for the Liturgy. Any Sunday School teacher should remember how such grammatical mutilation was rejected in Gaul in 586 by the Council of Mâcon, coincident with the death of the last pagan Visigothic ruler in Spain, Leovigildo, a man of unenlightened attitudes toward women, and toward men too, for that matter. The Council's decision that male and female are both included in the term "man" was pronounced precisely 1400 years before the nuclear accident in Chernobyl to which

much infertility in Ukraine has subsequently been attributed. Someone identified as a spokesperson for the American bishops said that the neuterizing of pronouns would not apply to "vertical" language which, he (sic) explained to reporters, is language that goes up. I suppose one could choose the *via media* between horizontal and vertical language by keeping the texts as they are, but reading them at an angle. We might call it diagonal language. But the whole business seems ill-advised and could geld both God and man once we confront the Word Made Flesh. That, after all, was the perplexity of Monophysites like Eutyches (ca. 375–454) whose God, like the Duke of York's army in the children's rhyme, was "neither up nor down." I do not think it was a coincidence that Eutyches's advocate in the Byzantine court was a eunuch, Chrysaphius.

Most people are too astute to be taken in by gender muddling, although the Welsh in their childlike susceptibility thought ochre-stained bones of a man uncovered in 1823 were the "Red Lady of Paviland." Until the current gender-inclusive debate, the Church disapproved of gelding humans, but there were a lot of *castrati*, or *evirati*, in Italy and they even sang in the Vatican. Prior to the use of castrati in the Sistine Chapel in the seventeenth century, use was made of falsettist male sopranos whose voices were trained by a secret Spanish method which did not involve mutilation and which evidently was at least as old as the Visigothic courts of such as Leovigildo. There has been a revival of interest today in these *sopranisti* or "counter-tenors"; their reception has been diminished by critics who complain not that they sound as though they have been castrated, but that they sound as though they are being castrated. There is no record of the aforementioned Leovigildo's musical tastes, but they could hardly have been more confined than those of his far-distant successor on the Spanish throne, Philip V, who required the eunuch Carlo "Il Ragazzo" Farinelli to sing the same four songs night after night in the Escorial, and rewarded the mutant's monotony by giving him enormous political power, rather like that of Chrysaphius. Just once in competition did any male hit a higher note than Farinelli: Antonio Bernacchi, born in the same year as Handel, who brought him to London. On the 1150th anniversary of the Council of Mâcon, Bernacchi started a voice school in Bologna, near Farinelli's castle. While Bernacchi perforce had no progeny, his family name descended upon the Tasmanian seismologist Louis Charles Bernacchi, who completed his journey to Antarctica with Scott and set out to explore British Namaqualand on the two hundredth anniversary of Philip V's loss of Gibraltar to England. The eunuch Giovanni Battista

Velluti sang in the opera *Seria* in Berlin in 1811, which just happened to be the 3000th anniversary of the death of the Pharaoh Siptah of Egypt, who had many neutered courtiers. Velluti was almost as popular in his day as is the crooner Michael Jackson, a lapsed member of the sub-Eutychian cult known as Jehovah's Witnesses. He performed in London in 1829 where the last of the celebrity castrati, Pergetti, sang in 1844 during the state visit of Czar Nicholas I. St. Alphonsus Liguori records different opinions about eunuchs among theologians, but until now the Church never had a de-sexed Liturgy.

The most pertinent scriptural reference for gender-inclusivity is the Ethiopian Eunuch of Acts 8. As the Eastern rites include a Liturgy of St. John Chrysostom and a Liturgy of St. James, the Western rite could be altered to a Liturgy of the Ethiopian Eunuch. But to do so would discredit that fine man, for he never asked Philip to neuterize the Book of Isaiah. Moreover, it is certain that so highly educated a member of the court of Queen Candace never spoke an oriental version of Ebonics.

MY MILLION
MAN SPEECH

I DID NOT ATTEND THE ORATION DELIVERED DURING THE
Million Man March in 1995 by the Nation of Islam cleric,
Louis Farrakhan. A prominent "supply-side" economist called it
a "magnificent speech." Anyone interested in coincidences
would have to agree. Minister Farrakhan's powers of association
are acute. Over the course of several hours, he multiplied scintillating observations, such as the indisputable fact that, if we
put a "1" in front of the number 555 which represents the
height in feet of the Washington Monument, we get 1555. He
went on to claim that 1555 was the year that slaves were first
brought to Jamestown, Virginia. In this, he was off by at least
52 years, but I suspect this may have been a rhetorical device to
prod our memories into recalling that in the year 52 A.D. the
notorious slavemaster Vologases I became Emperor of the
Parthians.

Minister Farrakhan dazzled the crowd, and presumably the
aforementioned "supply-side" economist, by announcing that
the statues of Jefferson and Lincoln in the District of Columbia

are each nineteen feet tall, and that Jefferson was the third President and Lincoln the sixteenth, the sum of which is nineteen. Then he chanted: "What is so deep about this number 19?" The 9 in 19 represents the months that all of us, except the premature, spent in the womb. And what about the 1 before the 9 without which it would not be 19? Well, "it means that there's something secret that has to be unfolded." The effect on the "million men" on the Mall was electric.

Those whose powers of association are less honed than the epideictic clergyman's will have to acknowledge the power of coincidences to enthrall a crowd. None of our recent presidents has matched Farrakhan's gift. George Herbert Walker Bush, I believe, in a spontaneous moment told reporters that he had been born on his own birthday, but such a weak try will get no one a niche in the Pantheon of Coincidentalists. James Earl Carter could have enlivened his first baleful State of the Union address in 1978 by informing the joint houses that he was speaking on the one thousandth anniversary of the accession of King Ethelred the Unready. His critics probably would have exploited that detail for partisan purposes. Nor would they have failed to draw a comparison between Ethelred's flight to Rouen at the approach of Sweyn and Carter's return to Plains, Georgia after the election of Ronald Reagan. Connoisseurs of Thomas Gainsborough's canvass "The Blue Boy", which was painted to challenge a canon of the Royal Academy against the use of blue as a thematic color, will appreciate this: Sweyn's father was Henry Bluetooth and he died in 1014 in the village of Gainsborough. My impression is that Minister Farrakhan's information of Ethelred, or any of the Cerdic line of Saxons, is tenuous; yet some similar reference could have made his speech even more magnificent in the estimation of the aforementioned "supply-side" economist.

Should I ever face an audience of a million men in the nation's capital, I would shout into the microphone portentous puzzles that escaped the attention even of Minister Farrakhan. I picture myself wiping my brow as I tell all those amiable and eager faces that the expenses and receipts of the Glasgow World Exposition of 1901 were absolutely identical. The applause subsides and my bodyguard draws closer as I look to heaven and cry out that the arithmetic sum of the years of Czar Alexander II's birth and death (1818 and 1881) are the same, and that he was assassinated by a bomb thrower exactly as the French Egyptologist, Gaston Maspero (1846–1916), was uncovering the royal mummies at Deir el-Bahri. Caught up on a tide of appreciative murmurs, I cover my face with trembling hands and scream that the septic influenza epidemic which swept large portions of the world from 1917 to 1919 killed 27 million people: a figure precisely one thousand times the size in square miles of Lake Victoria in Africa. Having waited dramatically for the clapping to stop, I smilingly reveal that thermoelectric pyrometers contain an alloy of platinum made of 18 percent rhodium, which is the very same percentage by which the population of Lexington, Kentucky increased between 1910 and 1920; and that the arithmetic sum of the year of the financial "Panic of 1873" following the collapse of Jay Cooke's bank matches the arithmetic sum of the year the Society of the Cincinnati was founded in Newburgh, New York. As a million voices rise in frenzied ecstasy, I bellow in a final flourish: "The 8,000,000 members of the Methodist Church when it united three of its branches on May 5, 1939 were exactly twice the number of bushels of grain destroyed when a Chicago grain elevator burned six days later." With hands raised in patriarchal blessing I sob: "The Eucalyptus attains a maximum height of 250 feet, equal to the 250 acres covered by Timpanogo's Cave in Utah, which means there's something secret that has to be unfolded."

Then hoarse and weary, I await the reviews of my speech by the more astute journalists and intellectuals who know a magnificent speech when it trickles down to them. They would include, naturally, the above-mentioned supply-side economist and all the astonished media commentators who tried to put a positive spin on the Million Man March, which was rather like ignoring the speeches at the old Nuremberg rallies and admiring instead the orderly crowds and colorful bunting.

A VARIETY OF SPIRITS

FOR TWENTY-FIVE YEARS, FRANCISCO MORALES deli-vered milk to the lactarians of El Paso, Texas. This "Pancho", who died in 1997 at the age of seventy-eight, was the father of the adult beverage known as the "margarita." Milk and margar-itas do not combine. Many of us as children learned the nursery adage, "contraria contrariis curantur": the principle that oppo-sites are cured by opposites, which is the foundation of allo-pathic medicine. Pancho was not an allopathist. He may have become a milkman because our society, which overpays basket-ball stars and rock singers, makes no provision for the inventors of important drinks.

Crapulence proposes more coincidences than may in fact exist, but the real ones are fascinating enough. Take the case, as it were, of the suffragette president of Bryn Mawr College, M. Carey Thomas. Her name was Martha, but she disdained its docile connotations. A respected scholar and administrator mighty in her bulwarks, she was a lapsed Quaker, although it is not clear how that is determined. Dr. Thomas was not related to André Antoine Thomas, the philologist who co-authored the *Dictionnaire Général de la Langue Francaise*, but both were born in 1857, and died in 1935 at the same age as Pancho Morales, who died on the fiftieth anniversary of the death of Wayne Bidwell Wheeler, general counsel of the Anti-Saloon League and author of the prohibitionist Volstead Act. In their birth-year, another Thomas, called Jerry, a bartender at the Occidental Hotel in San Francisco, invented the "martini", which he named for the town of Martinez in California.

André Antoine Thomas probably kept to wine, and there is no record of M. Carey Thomas tasting one of Jerry Thomas's inventions, although many around her must have. One thing we do know, and its symmetry is compelling: as the year of the birth of the two academic Thomases saw the birth of the martini, the year of their death launched, on June 10, Alcoholics Anonymous.

Königsburg beer has become popular in the United States even among many people who have no interest in Immanuel Kant. That hydropot philosopher of strict habits was born in Königsburg in 1724 and died there in 1804 as the United States Federal District Judge, John Pickering (1777–1846), was being convicted of drunkenness and profanity. Precisely 110 years later, the British destroyed a German cruiser in the Rufiji River in German East Africa, which vessel was named for Kant's city and was laden with quantities of its beer.

She sank nineteen years after the Anti-Saloon League was founded, which was also the date (December 17, 1895) on which President Grover Cleveland proposed a toast to a commission which fixed a boundary between Venezuela and British Guiana. The Anti-Saloon League was a more dour version of the Total Abstinence Society founded by the Capuchin priest from Tipperary, Theobald Mathew (1790–1856). Bishop John Hughes of New York sniffed heresy in the very name Total Abstinence. Besides Mathew's work among the Irish, this thaumaturge pledged nearly 100,000 Scotsmen to sobriety and then went to America where in 1849 he gave the pledge to President Polk, whom Sam Houston would call a victim of the use of water as a beverage. Father Mathew changed the course of history by also giving the pledge to the future President Fillmore, who kept his name.

Older than the first Königsburg brewery is the Spartanburg brewery of Munich, where monks began producing malt beer in 1397. Exactly five hundred years later, Nancy Langhorne married her first husband; when this teetotaling prohibitionist became the Viscountess Astor, she had a social secretary named Miss Brew. "Pancho" Morales died in the six hundredth anniversary year of the Spartanburg brewery. In the same year of 1397 at Calais, King Richard II was probably complicit in the murder of Thomas of Woodstock, the Duke of Gloucester. Five hundred and forty years later, the unforgivably sober Prime Minister Neville Chamberlain signed the Munich Agreement, with the approbation of King George VI who was benevolent toward his own Duke of Gloucester, Henry, in spite of the

Duke's eccentric refusal to use ash trays for his cigars during frequent and extended cocktail hours. Gloucester, having resigned as governor-general of Australia on the centenary of the death of besotted Judge Pickering, would not have thought congenial the society of Father Mathew.

Rudely toward one of their collateral antecedents, a drink has been dubbed the "Bloody Mary." This perpetuates an extravagant prejudice, but it is some sort of tribute to the vitality of her religion. No one would think of calling a cocktail the "Westminster Confession" or an aperitif an "Albigensian." A basic instinct stays the imagination from nicknaming a cordial for John Calvin. It says something valiant for the religion of Mary Tudor, that Champagne and Chartreuse and Benedictine were the inventions of Dom Perignon (1638–1715) and other monks pursuing a life of perfection. Hennessy brandy was the inestimable benefaction of an Irish-Catholic émigré to France. So too was Haut Brion claret, which was spelled "Ho Bryen" by Samuel Pepys (1633–1703), whose foremost biographer, in an example of "contraria contrariis curantur", was John Drinkwater (1882–1937).

THE ROSWELL
INCIDENT

Proponents of the theory that aliens from outer-space crashed in Roswell, New Mexico in June of 1947, were encouraged by the extravagant efforts of the Pentagon to prove a fraud. In a press conference on June 25, 1997, military officials explained the event as the collapse of a weather balloon filled with mannequins. Even more counter-productive was the Air Force's attempt to persuade the Roswellians that a creature they saw, with a bulbous head and odd eyes, was a certain Captain Daniel Fulgham, with a bandaged head and face swollen from injuries in a balloon flight twelve years later. This would be like the Archbishop of Canterbury using Charles Laughton to disprove the existence of Henry VIII.

It seems suspicious that the year 1947 should have seen so many unsettling events in the United States: tornadoes in Texas, Oklahoma, and Kansas killing 167 persons; a ship explosion destroying most of Texas City; the death of 80 Northeasterners in a blizzard; and the singing debut of Margaret Truman with the Detroit Symphony Orchestra. At least the Pentagon

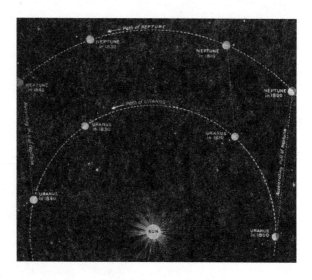

did not pretend that all of these were mannequins. In 1997, the only earthling who had authority to tell the full truth of the Roswell enigma was the President of the United States, who at the time of the sightings was an infant in Arkansas, which was the only state where nothing occurred on the day of the Roswell crash. Nor can we feel reassured by the knowledge that his vice president, Albert Gore, was born exactly nine months after the alleged extraterrestrial invasion. They were elected for a second term by 43 percent of the voters, almost exactly the portion of Americans who believe that a UFO crashed in New Mexico.

Coming at a time when the military is demoralized by scandals involving gender issues, a controversy about Martians can only test nerves that are already raw. Sexual preference is a hot enough topic without introducing planet preference. For this reason I am almost loathe to point out that the Roswell crash occurred on the tenth anniversary of the death of the philanthropic Boston banker Charles Hayden, for whom the Hayden planetarium in New York is named. The Roswellians, prudently imputing superior intelligence to strangers, might become more exercised to learn that Hayden was born in 1870; for in that year, John and Isaiah Hyatt patented celluloid which, while intended by them as a substitute for ivory in billiard balls, was part of that balloon material the Air Force claimed landed in Roswell. Parenthetically, that year was the one thousandth anniversary of the birth of the Arab astronomer and Hellenophile philosopher, Muhammad ibn-Muhammad ibn-Tarkhan ibn Uzalagh al-Farabi, more recognizable to us as Alfarabius.

Like Captain Fulghum, the unswollen Jonathan Swift (1667–1745) once was mistaken for an extraterrestrial being. The reason is riveting. In the third book of his *Gulliver's Travels* published in 1726, he describes the astronomers on the flying island of Laputa engaged in arcane pursuits such as "a project for extracting sun-beams out of cucumbers, which were to be put into vials hermetically sealed and let out to warm the air in raw inclement summers." But these rarified theoreticians also contemplate two moons of Mars. The description exactly fits the two satellites Deimos and Phobos which were not discovered until 151 years later by Asaph Hall (1829–1907) who was professor of mathematics at the United States Naval Observatory in Washington, D.C. Hall's corroboration of Swift in August of 1877 led some fantasyists to conjecture that Swift had used privileged information from another natal planet.

One more intriguing coincidence attaches to the discovery of the position of the planet Neptune simultaneously in 1846 by John Couch Adams (1819–1892) in England and Urbain Jean Joseph Leverrier (1811–1877) in France, each working independently. Both relied on calculations based on the perturbations of Uranus, which was discovered on March 13, 1781 by the father of sidereal science, Sir Friedrich Wilhelm Herschel (1738–1822), who described the existence of the motion of binary stars.

There is a warning in this. Herschel first named Uranus after George III: "Georgium Sidus." Herschel had originally been a music teacher. The king's own fondness for music and stargazing was surpassed only by his interest in clocks, and he became increasingly obsessed with both as his porphyritic dementia worsened. The royal malady was made all the more poignant by the fact that the king's father had defended General Wolfe against imputations of madness. His court began to suspect that he might be one sandwich short of a picnic on that fatal day in 1788 when he got out of his carriage in Windsor Park and began to speak to an oak tree under the mistaken impression that it was his cousin, the King of Prussia. On the centenary of this lunacy, in Iowa, Belva Ann Lockwood was nominated by the Equal Rights Party to become the first woman to run for the presidency of the United States.

Armed with this information, the people of Roswell, the officials of the Pentagon, and the American taxpayers should draw a veil over the whole scene in New Mexico until some distant time when the full facts may reveal themselves. Poor King George had no such rational option. He spent his last days at his harpsichord, playing incessantly what Shelley in his *Epipsychidion* would call music "sweet as stops of planetary music heard in a trance."

LEND AN EAR

"IF YOU BITE HIM AGAIN, I'LL DISQUALIFY YOU." THUS spake the surprisingly contralto voice of Mills Lane, referee of the Michael Tyson–Evander Holyfield heavyweight boxing match in Nevada on June 28, 1997. Tyson had just bitten off part of Holyfield's ear in violation of the Marquis of Queensbury Rules, as the Prince of Wales was resting aboard the royal yacht "Britannia" before returning Hong Kong to China. One hundred years earlier, Germany acquired Kiaochow leading to the formation of "The Society of Harmonious Fists", known as the "Boxers", while back in Nevada, James "Gentleman Jim" Corbett (1866–1933) lost the heavyweight title to Robert Prometheus Fitzsimmons (1862–1917). Corbett died on the fiftieth anniversary of the death of John Graham Chambers, the actual author of the boxing rules named for the eighth Marquis of Queensbury.

The Tyson frenzy was a golden moment, forever lost, for sports commentators to invoke the shade of the bully, Sir Thomas Styles, who, similarly had attacked the poet Shelley while at Eton. Years later, on his way to join Wellington's forces in the Peninsular War, Styles was so driven to distraction by

fleas in Portugal that he committed suicide. A harsh and humiliating fate this, and rather gratuitous since the Queensbury Rules were not drawn up until 1867.

According to the New York Department of Health, in 1996 the number of people partially chewed by other people in Brooklyn was 419. This figure matches the year of St. Boniface's recognition as pope by the Emperor Honorius. Manhattanites seem to be of a calmer frame of mind, for in the same year only 175 of them were bitten, matching the year in which Pope St. Soter was chewed to death by animals according to oral tradition. Bites of many sorts can be fatal. King Alexander of Greece, the second son of the deposed King Constantine, died on October 25, 1920 from blood poisoning after having been bitten by his pet monkey. Holyfield survived his wound, unlike the Scottish pugilist Sandy MacKay, who died in the ring after the forty-seventh round against the Irishman Simon Byrne in 1830, forty-seven years before Queen Victoria succumbed to the flatteries of Disraeli and accepted the Crown Imperial. As MacKay lay dying, a baby was born who would be known to the world as Alfred William Howitt, the anthropologist of the aboriginals of Australia and anthropophagists of New Zealand who considered human ears a delicacy. Robert Prometheus Fitzsimmons grew up in New Zealand, having emigrated from Cornwall. As the great Howitt died in 1908, John "Jack" Johnson delivered the winning punch to Thomas Burns for the world heavyweight championship in Sydney. All this is by way of coincidence within coincidence, for the father of the eponymous first Viscount Sydney, died in the same year that the eighth Marquis of Queensbury stepped down as representative peer for Scotland.

These magical figures could easily distract us from the issue at hand. The usual gang of emetic social engineers flaccidly used Tyson's mordant act as an excuse to decry all contact sports as incubators of blood lust. My complaint is verily the opposite: what neurasthenic weaklings they were who stampeded out of the Las Vegas arena on June 28 at the sight of a small bit of ear. Forty-three boxing fans were injured in the stampede: coincidentally, one for each of the pretended years of the rich attorney's elderly ugly daughter in *Trial by Jury*. Did Caligula's mobs flee the Colosseum as more than earlobes flew about? Horace calmly wrote poetic odes as mortal men challenged rhinoceroses in Flavian's amphitheater. Pugilism actually unmasks the squeamishness of Americans, like many of our political leaders and jurists who are "horrified" by the dismemberment of anyone larger than an infant. The whole chaotic scene in Las Vegas must have reminded many of Vincenzo dei Rossi's ridiculous statue of Hercules and Diomedes wrestling, now in the Palazzo Vecchio of Florence.

Violence vests in different guises. Backbiting can be more painful than ear biting, yet the intelligentsia backbite as a habit. In the final round, the chattering classes draw more blood than the chomping classes. It has been said that university politics are so vicious because the stakes are so small. That surely is so from the monetary angle. Tyson would have been paid for his brief bout 606 times the average annual salary of a university professor. Perhaps teachers would be paid more if they publicly chewed those with whom they disagree.

The wife of Mr. Holyfield is a physician, specializing in pain management—an Orwellian term but a welcome thing nonetheless. To be so espoused is a happy situation, but supine decadents would even replace male boxers with women, like the 106-pound Golden Gloves champion, Jill ("The Zion Lion") Matthews. One reason I oppose combat duty for women is not that they are weak, but that they tend to be more violent than men in any arena, including the political. Women therefore have to exercise even more self-control than men, and thus can teach men much about deportment, but only by heroic effort.

There is the phenomenal case of France's illustrious female concert pianist of the nineteenth century, Madame L'Oreille. Since her name means "ear", it is all the more poignant that she was born with no outer ears. Because of an unusual structure of her inner ear, which has been explained to me by a friend who is perhaps the world's foremost audiologist, she was able to hear by keeping her mouth wide open. Hers was a physical instance of the more problematic moral instance of those who compensate for moral deafness by not shutting their mouths.

THE CRADLES OF 1809

REGARDLESS OF HOW FREQUENTLY WE HAVE BEEN IN-spired by the parliamentary exchanges between Thomas Babington Macaulay and William Ewart Gladstone on the civil disabilities of Jews, one more reading is never enough. Although Macaulay had the upper hand morally as well as rhetorically in the instance, as he also had in the earlier debate on slavery in the West Indies, he wrote in 1830 with equal application to the United States: "We know no spectacle so ridiculous as the British public in one of its periodical fits of morality." We shall have no such fits. Our subject is style.

Gladstone deplored the state, almost sacrosanct in modern politics, when "appearance annexes to substance", but that does not discount appearance altogether. In his "Essay on Athenian Orators", Macaulay insisted that the object of oratory is not truth alone, but persuasion. And here I may be bowdlerizing him the way Luther did the Epistle of James, for Macaulay actually did not say "truth alone" but "truth." His maxim may still hold, even though he was aware in another essay on Machiavelli that nothing is so useless as a maxim. Nothing is so useful as a maxim then to the bibliobibulist in his search for useless information. The clergyman Sydney Smith was succinct: "(Macaulay) not only overflowed with learning, but stood in the slop."

The artistry of Macaulay and Gladstone thrills in the same revelation that makes what passes for persuasion in our day seem damp as a sponge at the bottom of a lukewarm bath. Who today in Congress could describe an air strike on Serbia the way Macaulay described the Battle of Naseby?

"And the Man of Blood was there, with his long essenced hair,
And Astley, and Sir Marmaduke, and Rupert of the Rhine."

Our age has no senator to speak of Libyan terrorists as Gladstone spoke sonorously of the Turks: ". . . one and all, bag and baggage, shall I hope, clear out from the province they have desolated and profaned." In descant to their decibels, modern words belched in congressional hearings and academic assemblies are anemic aubades trilled on warped and whining flutes.

Gladstone was born in 1809, nine years Macaulay's junior. The year is sanguineous in the popular imagination: conjuring up the Battle of Wagram and the Massacre of the Mamelukes, let alone the Warsaw army's conquest of Galicia, Turkish strife with Russia, and Sweden's loss of Finland. Today it is all too easy for the ordinary citizen to confuse 1809's achievement of the Treaty of Amritsar with the Riots of Amritsar which happened 110 years later. The brilliant fact is that 1809 gave rise to pens mightier than swords. Gladstone's infant voice was not the only prodigy of the year that heard the newborn cries of Alfred Tennyson, Edgar Allan Poe, Oliver Wendell Holmes, Felix Mendelssohn, Charles Darwin, and Abraham Lincoln.

Let the infants of 1809 mature. In the year 1839 of the Macaulay-Gladstone debates, Tennyson was finishing *Locksley Hall*, Poe was preparing the *Tales of the Grotesque and Arabesque*, Holmes was teaching anatomy at Dartmouth College, Mendelssohn was conducting the Gewandhaus concerts in Leipzig, Darwin was marrying his cousin, and Lincoln was practicing law. Lincoln, who would cruelly be caricatured by cartoonists as an ape, shared his birthday of February 12 in 1809 with the quixotic author of *The Descent of Man*. And Lincoln's years spent in New Salem, Illinois as a store clerk, mill manager, and rail splitter while educating himself, courting Ann Rutledge, and keeping a pet hound (1831–1837), were almost exactly coterminous with Darwin's expedition on the "Beagle" to South America and Australasia.

The birth of all these men *simul et simul* is too much for albuminous sociologists to brush off. If they had all cried from the same nursery in the same land, one might trace their genius to the milk and their style to the air salubrious. That is not the way it was. Whatever it was, its voices poured out speeches and rhymes and music of empyreal cast. Gladstone was the last of them to die, in 1898, and when he did there was mold on the cradles of civilization: the Swiss nationalized their railways and Norway granted suffrage for everyone except women. Only Teddy Roosevelt's charge up San Juan Hill, the establishment of the National Institute of Arts and Letters, and the birth of C. S. Lewis, rescued 1898 from complete ignominy. A cacophonous century later, the great grown ghosts of 1809 loom in terrible judgment over politicians who whine their muddy diction, and sham poets who slur doggerel on public occasions, and pithecoid rock singers who screech and scratch and find no finale. Style is dead.

Peeking into the cradles of 1809, one invokes William Johnson Cory's translation of the epitaph on Heraclitus by Callimachus

How often you and I
Had tired the sun with talking and sent him down the sky.

Still, the pleasant voices of such ghosts lift in the wind like nightingales. "For death he taketh all away / But them he cannot take." Cory, like Tennyson, died in 1892, two years before Gladstone's queen dismissed him with a brief chat about the weather and no thanks for the years that had turned him grey. *Acta est fabula*. Or as some of our modern orators might put it, "Lays 'n gennelmin, ya know, that's the way iddis."

WE BAND OF
BROTHERS

BERNARD SEVERIN INGEMANN'S BELOVED DANISH HYMN
"Igjennem Nat og Traengsel", written in 1825, was published
twenty-four years later in the *Nyt Tillaeg til Evangelisk-Christelig
Psalmebog* and did not appear in English for yet another eight
years. The translator, Sabine Baring-Gould, was prolific even
for an English vicar. Born in 1834 when the Seminoles were
evicted from Florida, and dying in 1924 one month before Ira
Gershwin's brother George first performed his "Rhapsody in
Blue" with the Paul Whiteman Orchestra, his long life produced dozens of books including the 15-volume *Lives of the
Saints* which in its morocco-bound edition has been a decora-
tive element in many rectories. He completed a *Book of Were-
wolves* in the same year that he wrote "Onward Christian
Soldiers" for a children's festival at Horbury Bridge.

Baring-Gould's English version of "Igjennem Nat og
Traengsel" sings: "Brother clasps the hand of brother / Stepping
fearless through the night." Spiritual brotherhood draws its im-
agery from biological brotherhood which, by definition, is

coincidental and supplies an inexhaustible lode of secondary coincidences. Just consider, for example, how St. Paul was dismissed by the Roman proconsul of Achaia, Junius Annaeus Gallio (alias Marcus Annaeus Novatus), a biological brother of the Stoic philosopher Lucius Annaeus Seneca, whose signature name is the same as the Iroquoian tribe inhabiting North America

ica like the Seminoles, but farther north (cf. Acts 18: 12–17). St. Paul and Seneca were killed by order of the same man: Lucius Domitius Ahenobarbus, known to us as the emperor Nero. Seneca had been Nero's teacher but Nero decided he could teach himself. This was a dangerous business, for since he apparently thought teachers should be killed, he killed himself.

Philosophically, Seneca was a remote and more refined precursor of Jeremy Bentham, whose extravagant promotion of utilitarianism overshadowed his botanist brother George's studies of the flora of Hong Kong. Another brother, Sir Samuel, was a colonel in the Russian naval service. Samuel's tenure as supervisor of the shipyard in Kritchev coincided with the years John Paul Jones spent with the Russian navy on the Black Sea from 1788 to 1790. At this time, another naval officer congenially named Richard Brothers was promoting himself as heir to the British throne on the strength of his claim that he was a direct descendant of King David; his own brothers had him confined to a lunatic asylum until 1806. John Paul Jones's flagship, the *Bonhomme Richard* was named in tribute to Benjamin Franklin. Ben's name is almost as inseparable from the City of Brotherly Love as is William Penn whose portrait in the great hall of Christ Church in Oxford bespeaks a most glorious irony: the future Quaker is the only one in that vast gallery depicted in armor. He was a son of Admiral Sir William Penn whose naval victory over the Dutch at Lowestoft, coincidentally, was won on the 1600th anniversary of the death of Seneca.

This brings to mind the ship designer and co-inventor of the armored tank, Sir Eustace Tennyson-D'Eyncourt, a second cousin of Alfred, Lord Tennyson whose brother Charles joined him in publishing *Poems by Two Brothers*. Sir Eustace assumed the admiralty in 1912, as Robert Love Taylor was dying in Tennessee where his own marplot brother Alfred had run against him for the governorship in 1886. Actually, they campaigned in good fun as one might expect of brothers born in a place called Happy Valley, fiddling and joshing each other on the campaign platform.

Anyone who flies kites or encourages others to do so knows that the founder of the Boy Scouts, Lord Baden-Powell of Gilwell, was a brother of Baden Fletcher Smyth who invented a man-lifting kite in 1894. Another brother, Sir George, helped write the constitution for Malta seven years earlier. The adventures of these brothers, from the West Indies to Matabeleland, were matched only by the Meyer brothers: Hans, the first German to climb Mt. Kilimanjaro, and Hermann, the first German to explore the Atelchu tributary of the Ronuro River in Brazil.

Those who prefer skates to kites will remark that two of the most venerable writers to figure skate were the Dean of St.

Paul's, William Ralph Inge, and Edward Frederic Benson, the author of more than a hundred sundry books and a promoter of world-class skating competitions. Each had four brothers, one of Edward's being the writer, Monsignor Robert Hugh Benson. His brother Arthur, author of the text for "Pomp and Circumstance", had been Assistant Headmaster at Eton along with William Inge whose brother Charles joined Edward in excavating the Thersilion at Megalopolis in 1892.

These clerical connections recall the family of Edmund Arbuthnott Knox, whose sons included the incomparable Monsignor Ronald Knox and Wilfrid, a distinguished presence in Cambridge University for many years and promoter of the Advent "Lessons and Carols." From 1903 to 1921, Edmund was Anglican Bishop of Manchester where, in 1799, Robert Owen had purchased the New Lanark mills in partnership with the above mentioned Jeremy Bentham. Owen became so very rich that he could afford to become a socialist. With the tenuous practicality of his Welsh blood, he decided to set up a Utopia in Indiana where all would live in brotherly peace on secular principles. His community of New Harmony lasted from 1825 (the year Ingemann wrote his hymn) to 1828 and nearly bankrupted him. By the age of 82, Owen was so impoverished that he turned from socialism to spiritualism. The tragedy was needless, if only his mental nudity had better understood how spiritual brotherhood needs a Spirit higher than altruism to work. Too bad he died nine years before the translation of "Igjennem Nat og Traengsel."

THE TIME OF THE SINGING OF BIRDS

Any normal teenager who daydreams of becoming a famous feuilletonist will find no theme more promising than the coincidence of men and birds. Wild or domesticated or table fare, there has never been a high achievement without birds in hand or bush or sky above. Keats's fleet nightingale and Coleridge's fetid albatross conspire and never go away.

On January 10, 236, a dove settled on the head of the previously inconspicuous Fabian, and, the Roman clergy took it as a sign that he should succeed Anterus as pope. In June of 1846, a dove perched on the coach of Giovanni Cardinal Mastai-Ferretti, Bishop of Imola in the Romagna, who was passing through Fossombrone on his way to the conclave gathering to elect a successor to Pope Gregory XVI. Although the Papal Secretary of State, Luigi Cardinal Lambruschini was thought the most *papabile*, Mastai-Ferretti became Pope Pius IX. When Angelo Cardinal Roncalli was Papal Nuncio to Paris (1944–1953), a dove circled around his head during a pilgrimage to Lourdes, an event recalled when he became Pope John

XXIII in 1958, the centenary of the commencement of a medical practice in Bombay by the Anglo-Indian physiophilist, Sir George Birdwood. Roncalli's tenure in Paris concluded on the 700th anniversary of the traditional date for the first well-known song about birds in English literature:

> Sumer is icumen in,
> Lhude sing cuccu!
> Groweth sed, and bloweth med,
> And springth the wude nu.

The College of Cardinals elected the della Genga pope, Leo XII, in the hope that he would lead a reform of the papacy and the papal states, but he was something of a disappointment, and the first hint that this would be so came when he started shooting birds in the Vatican gardens for relaxation. His claim to a place in the records of coincidence is by way of having been born in 1760 and crowned pope in 1823, which years have an identical arithmetic sum. Captious curmudgeons link Catholic cardinals with the sixth horn of the Dragon in the Apocalpyse. Cardinals are more happily associated with the crested finch, *Richmondena cardinalis*. There is the winsome story of the valiant anti-slave crusader, Charles Martial Cardinal Allemand-Lavigerie who, as archbishop of Algiers, dismissed the objections of the French Consul General and married Prince Si Ahmed Tidjani, a religious leader in southern Algeria, to Aurelie Picard in 1871. The Prince, visiting Bordeaux, fell in love when he saw the housekeeper to Postmaster General Steenacker feeding pigeons. As the prince and the pigeon girl were wed, feudalism was abolished in Japan.

Another romantic saga links the homely chicken and lilting canary. Chicken Marengo was a dish concocted of the few available items during the Battle of Marengo in 1800, which was the reference in Sherlock Holmes's noble line: "We have not yet met our Waterloo, Watson, but this is our Marengo." Conspicuous in that battle was Maurice Dupin, a grandson of Marshal Maurice de Saxe who was the most illustrious of the 360 illegitimate children of Augustus II "The Strong" of Saxony and Poland. Maurice married Sophie Delaborde, the daughter of a Parisian canary peddler, one month before the birth of a girl Aurore, the future virvestite Baroness Dudevant known by the pen name George Sand. Her friend Flaubert would create "Loulou", the most notorious parrot in literature.

In 1810, the year of the birth of Sand's lover Chopin, a clown named Barry of Astley's circus in London floated down the Thames as a publicity stunt in a washtub pulled by geese dressed in ribbons. As the spectacle was unfolding, the Father of the American Circus, Phineas Taylor Barnum, serendipitously entered the world in Bethel, Connecticut. The term "serendipity" was coined by Horace Walpole who kept an exotic aviary at his neo-Gothic castle outside Twickenham. His father's steward, John Wrott, hid the tenants' rents in dead geese for safety during transit from the family's estate in Lynn to their London house in Berkeley Street.

Into this chirping pastorale, a gloomier note intrudes. The

year of Pope John XXIII's coronation less the number of Augustus II's illegitimate children is 1598: the birth year in Naples of the *wunderkind* Giovanni Lorenzo Bernini. When his portrait bust of King Charles I was unveiled in the garden of Greenwich Palace on August 15 in 1630, a hawk flew overhead with a rodent in its mouth, dropping a bit of blood directly on the neck of the sculpture. As omens go, this one was invested with awful significance when the king was beheaded on January 30, 1649. The wife of Edgar Allan Poe, author of "The Raven", died of tuberculosis on January 30 as well, in 1847; and Poe himself died two years later in the third centenary year of the king's calamity.

The year of Mrs. Poe's death was also the year of the birth of James Anthony Bailey who teamed up with Phineas Taylor Barnum. Rejoicing in the same family name was the naturalist Vernon Bailey, publisher in 1923 of *Beaver Habits, Beaver Control, and Possibilities in Beaver Farming*, a *vade mecum* for studying the rodent family *Castoridae*. His wife was Florence Merriam, whose *Birds Through an Opera Glass* in 1889 staked her claim as the leading ornithologist of western American wildfowl.

But the two most interesting items I know of birds is that their happiest trilling, at least the best I ever heard, was on the mount in Galilee where the Beatitudes were blessed; and one place where birds never sing or even perch is a patch of land in Verdun where war was infernal. This I cannot rank as coincidence.

ALL GAS AND GAITERS

IRONY WAS STRAINED AT THE UNITED NATIONS' "EARTH Summit" in 1997 when President Clinton, President Chirac, and Prime Minister Blair jointly issued a warning about the proliferation of gas. Long before, Charles Dickens coined the phrase "All gas and gaiters." In days when clergymen dressed better, gaiters were associated with the higher ranks of them, and it may be unfeeling though not irrational to link them, like politicians, with the kind of prolix twaddle for which gas is a vivid metaphor. Here in speaking of a link, I fear one commits a pun because the world's leading expert on gaseousness is Colin Leakey, whose name itself is a word play, and whose step-mother Mary Leakey discovered a jawbone in the Olduvai Gorge in Tanzania, which she thought might have belonged to the ephemeral "missing link." Her son's research into leaking gas has so far been more substantial. In the year of the UN Earth Summit, his invention of a "flatometer" that meas-ures the production of methane from digested high-fiber legumes, was granted a Royal Patent, making him even more conspicuous in the public eye than his conservationist brother Richard, who is known widely for his efforts to save the East African elephant.

Colin's arcane work has centered on the bean. The only Mr. Bean of whom I am aware in the cultural annals, besides Judge Roy Bean of western saga and the pseudonymous comedian and the actor Orson Bean, is Tarleton Hoffman Bean (1846–1916) who, strangely enough, was curator of the New York Aquarium. Bean's English contemporary was the ichthyologist Jonathan Couch, grandfather of Arthur Quiller-Couch, the literary critic who as an Oxford undergraduate occupied the former rooms of John Henry Newman in Trinity College. No one devoted more energy as an essayist to deflating bombastic and borborygmic speech than Quiller-Couch. In the year of Tarleton Bean's death, the Kaiser, having consented to the use of poison gas, appointed General Paul von Beneckendorff und von Hindenburg army chief-of-General-staff. The dirigible named in the general's honor blew up over Lakehurst, New Jersey in 1937 as the result of a leaky hydrogen gas valve. H. L. Mencken's *Treatise on Right and Wrong* was published coincidentally on the death of von Hindenburg in 1934; its author used many ingenious metonymies for methane in references to Eleanor Roosevelt.

Matilda Ayrton, foundress of a famous school for midwives in Japan in 1873, and Professor Bean were born in the same year. On the occasion of her birth, gas lighting was introduced in the Capitol in Washington and a gas explosion in the Karlsruhe Theater in St. Petersburg took two hundred lives. She died quietly in 1883 and her husband married Hertha, who pioneered the study of sand ripples and then invented the antigas

fan. As Hertha probably knew more than any woman of her day about the properties of nitrous oxide popularly known as "laughing gas", it is fascinating that her maiden name was the same as the Marx brothers, just as her antecedent Matilda's maiden name was the same as the comic actor Charles Spencer "Charlie" Chaplin.

Although Sir Robert Walpole, later first Earl of Orford, was born in 1676 only months before Stephen Hales who analyzed legumes in his *Vegetable Staticks* and invented an artificial ventilator, he was considerably less scientific in his obsession with internal eructations. While J. H. Plumb's masterful two essays on Walpole's wine cellars and kitchens are unsurpassed and render any domestic library without them incomplete, he neglects to mention this odd item: the atrabilious Earl blamed all his problems on gallstones and believed he could be cured by consuming a certain mathematical dosage of soap daily. By the time of his death, Walpole had consumed 180 carefully measured pounds of refined grease. Eighteen years later, Wolfgang

Coincidentally

Amadeus Mozart composed his first symphony while lodging in London at 180 Ebury Street. The significance of this may be gossamer, but it can be a welcome distraction when one is forced to sit through the next long-winded speech.

Like Yeats withdrawing to a gentle place when he wearied of the world's fanfaronades, all of us have moments when we want to rest where nature's quiet hum is more eloquent than the fumy speeches of a fuliginous world.

"I will arise and go now, and go to Innisfree,
And a small cabin build there, of clay and wattles made:
Nine bean-rows will I have there, a hive for the honey bee,
And live alone in the bee-loud glade.

Our age of e-mail and websites is also an age of logorrhea. All communication and no communion. If the gaiters are gone, the rhetorical gas is gassier than ever. Clerics of every profession fill more journals and hold more conferences than the mind of man needs. Perhaps our age has entered its old age, like Shakespeare's senile man who "pipes and whistles in his sound." Verbosity and inanity go together, and were I to write more, I should only prove my point.

A CAVALCADE OF GEORGES

FEW LITERARY CONVENTIONS ARE MORE USEFUL THAN quotations of Aristotle when in a pinch. He gives a sheen to what might otherwise pass for inanity, especially when you do not know with perfect assurance what you are talking about. So we invoke his resolution: "It is the mark of an educated man to rest satisfied with the degree of precision which the nature of the subject admits and not to seek exactness where only an approximation is possible." Here is the formula for successful historians and unsuccessful politicians.

The maxim came to mind recently when I, seeking relief from the raucous publicity of another White House scandal, perused the Martyrology of Oengus. That Irish historian is as precise as he can be about the *megalomartyros* Saint George, and even more inexact when facts fail. Apparently, more nations, towns, churches and foundations invoke George as patron than any saint other than the Blessed Lady. By a blessed coincidence, he is my own patron. He is said to have appeared, along

with Saint Demetrius, to the first Crusaders when they defeated the Saracens at Antioch. The details of that remain inexact.

What is precisely true is that since the Crusades, soldiers have had an affinity for him. There is no evidence that General Custer kept a cult for George, but he bore his name, even as he rode into battle at Little Big Horn on June 25, 1876, outnumbered by the Sioux almost as greatly as Henry V was outnumbered by the French at Agincourt, though with less fortunate issue. We still thrill at the words of Shakespeare's king: "Shall not thou and I, between Saint Denis and Saint George, compound a boy, half-French, half-English, that shall go to Constantinople and take the Turk by the beard?" The bard's bearded Turk became a reality in the life, or more precisely the death, of

Custer. The Battle of Little Big Horn was coincident with the Bashi-Bazouk massacres in Bulgaria. A war correspondent, Januarius Aloysius MacGahan (1844–1870), covered the melancholy outrages of those tatterdemalion Turkish Irregulars, but he got little attention, even though the Bashi-Bazouks died in thousands and the Sioux scalped only 265; plus George the General.

Two years after the atrocities which MacGahan publicized in vain to excite American indignation, the Bulgarians' long-time Serbian rivals gained independence from the Turks, along with the Rumanians and Montenegrins. In 1815, to be precise, the governor of central Serbia, Milos Obrenovic (1780–1866) had begun a second revolt against the Turks, apparently unaware that simultaneously in England, the only daughter of the happily hapless George IV was being introduced to her future husband, Prince Leopold of Saxe-Coburg. Two years later, by a macabre coincidence, Princess Charlotte died in childbirth as Obrenovic was being proclaimed hereditary Prince of Serbia by the National Assembly. Charlotte's grandfather, George III, had lost his American colonies to George Washington, attaching an odd symmetry to Obrenovic's sobriquet: "the George Washington of Serbia." The title strains comparison, given Obrenovic's tendency to murder and pillage, and the way he plotted the assassination of the Serbs' chosen leader, Karageorge, or Czerny Djordje, which means "Black George." But so many Georges!

The Serbs are not a people with an unclouded history. On June 11, 1903, the sixteen-hundredth-anniversary year of the martyrdom of Saint George, inexactly configured, King Aleksander I Obrenovic and his wife Draga were assassinated along with fifty of their retinue. Draga's first husband was a Czech named Mashin, pronounced "machine" portentously inasmuch as the assassins of 1903 included members of the army corps of engineers. The autocrat Aleksander was succeeded by a grandson of Karageorge, Peter I Karageorgevich, at the same time Prince George of Greece (1867–1957) was serving as High Commissioner of Crete. Prince George died on the quincentenary of the death of King Ladislas of Bohemia. Ever faithful to the Georgian tradition, Jiri (George) of Podebrad (1420–1471) succeeded him.

Aristotle's philosophical champion in the papal court of the fifteenth century was George of Trebizond, secretary to Pope Paul II who excommunicated George of Podebrad in 1466 and fomented a crusade against him. From such a scene, one cannot help but invoke the meters of Milton:

> "And all who since, baptized or infidel
> Jousted in Aspramont or Montalban,
> Damasco, or Marocco, or Trebisond . . ."

Invoking the inexactitude commended by Aristotle, we may say that a lot of incidental Georges cross the chronicles of time, but there is exactly one George grand as he is mysterious. I recently saw an icon of him, several stories high, overlooking Red Square in Moscow where formerly a banner of Lenin had glared at his own tomb. And now there is also a valiantly garish statue on heroic height in the garden of the United Nations: George the Martyr casting his cross-topped lance into a dragon made of modern scrap weaponry. However many other Georges there have been, there is the one who is a soldier, and however endless the number of dragons may seem, in due time he puts an end to them all.

NAMES PROPER AND IMPROPER

AMONG THE BLITHE HABITS THAT BEFOG OUR CULTURE
as it careens toward wreckage, not crucial but annoying
nonetheless is the false and manipulative *bonhommie* of politicians using nicknames on formal occasions. There are presidents and prime ministers who want to be called Bill and Tony
and the like in documents and ceremonies. It reveals a self-con-
scious failure of humility. Tangential to this mistaken confusion
of pomp with pomposity is the lazy habit of altering names to
our convenience. Consider the widespread tendency to call
Cunobelinus Cymbeline and Boudicca Boadicea. Cymbeline
was the poeticized name given by Shakespeare to the Briton
king and father of Caractacus, or Caradawg according to the
listless labials of the Welsh. Here I risk offending the Bard, but
he did well mock the Welsh language in *Henry IV.-Part I* and
said that the devil understood it, which is probably why he
avoided it.

What the brave son of Cunobelinus failed to do in resisting
the Roman invasion led by Aulus Plautius (Ostorius Scapula

captured him in 50 A.D.), Boudicca accomplished as Queen of the Iceni. At least her alliance with the Trinobantes (Essex and Saxon Britons) kept the Romans at bay until 62 A.D. In retaliation for having been publicly flogged, she massacred 70,000 Britons who, as the Vichyites of their day, had collaborated with the invaders.

Boudicca would not have taken lightly the frilly alteration of her name to Boadicea. Nor is it possible to imagine the Romans being terrified by someone lispily named Cymbeline. Does a fierce name make a fierce fighter, or does the name seem fierce because it belongs to the fierce? It is similar to the conundrum case of pets: do owners start looking like their dogs, or do the owners (by subtle and subconscious self-projection) select dogs that resemble them? I cannot imagine Hitler playing with a chihuahua at Berchtesgaden, so I think it must be the latter.

As long as there are names, there will be misnomers. In the twentieth century we have had a Benito and a Fidel at whose baptisms the lustral waters could have boiled. In the larger scheme, though, it is hard to imagine a Placid the Hun or a Tinkerbelle the Conqueror.

The first wife of Evelyn Arthur St. John Waugh was also Evelyn, and friends avoided confusion by calling them He-Evelyn and She-Evelyn; but were they attracted by their names, or does the literary world remark their names only because they were attracted? The Englishman George Dance (1741–1825) and the Alsatian Jean Jacques Waltz (1873–1951) were painters; but do we match them because of their painting or because of the congruity of their professionally incongruous names? It is easy to remember that Alexander Pope was a Catholic, but it is confusing to learn that Cromwell's regimental commander against the Irish-Catholic rebels was George Monck (1608–1670) and that Joseph Priestley (1733–1804) promoted Unitarianism.

Was it because of his exemplary piety that we remember the name of the first Protestant Episcopal missionary to Africa? Or do we remember his name because it was Thomas Savage (1804–1880)? Or, indeed, did he become a missionary because of his name? Something in a name makes us pause when up against this fact: while England's greatest playwright was William Shakespeare, the only English pope to date was Nicholas Breakspeare (c.1100–1159).

The mathematician of Baghdad to whom we all owe so much, Muhammad ibn-Musa al-Khwarizmi (780–c.850), coined the term "al-jabr" (literally "the resetting of broken bones") for the mathematical system developed by the Hindu astronomer Brahmagupta (588–ca.660), and his own name gave us the term "algorism", designating decimal notation and the use of Arabic numerals. There would appear to be nothing curious or even coincidental about the labyrinthine evolution of algorism, until you realize that Vice President Al Gore, in matters of economics and fundraising and population statistics, often gets his figures wrong.

The builder of the first submarine capable of navigation in ocean depths was Simon Lake (1866–1945). The first American woman to ride into outer space, in the shuttle *Challenger* on June 18, 1983, was Sally K. Ride. The pioneering botanist and researcher of liverworts on potted plants was Thomas Potts James (1803–1882). And the inventor of a balance for measuring gravity was the German physicist Phillip von Jolly (1809–1884). I cannot prove that Mr. Lake would have stayed on dry land had he been Mr. Sands, or that Miss Ride would have led a quieter life with the name Walker. With a different moniker, Thomas Potts James might never have ventured into the entrancing world of potted liverworts, and Jolly might never have been driven by a perverse obstinacy to study gravity if he had been born into the family Grimm.

Dwelling further on these questions risks whimsy or pedantry, and dwelling interminably on them is the way of a lunacy whose only asylums are the madhouse and the university. Only one thing matters. The Apocalypse tells that at the last Great Assize, we shall finally see the meaning of our names on a white stone. That is to say, we shall know who we really are. What a man makes of his name, and not what his name makes of him, will determine whether the sight of that stone will petrify his very soul.

EGG TO APPLES

THE POPES WHO REIGNED IN FOURTEENTH-CENTURY Avignon have suffered at the hands of Francophobic chroniclers. They were an unusually sympathetic line of men, like Urban V (Guillaume de Grimoard), whose reforming instincts pleased few but got him beatified, and the aesthetic John XXII (Jacques d'Euse) who told Italian choristers to stop the vulgar and exhibitionist trilling of their voices. He was ignored. Clement VI (Pierre Roger de Beaufort) resembled the modern John XXIII in some ways. He promoted church unity, opposed Jew-baiters and was generally expansive and cheerful, if overly-optimistic about the course of events. In culinary sensibility, Pope Clement surpassed Pope John, who arranged his menus with anticipation and kept careful records of the Parmesan cheese industry. Although Clement's mystical powers were not acute, he enjoyed an almost preternatural talent for smelling sauces at long distances. This radiant fixture of the French papacy celebrated his coronation in 1342 with a menu of 1,023 sheep, 118 cows, 101 calves, 60 pigs, 10,471 hens, 914 kids, 300 pike, 1,446 geese, 50,000 cakes and 46,856 cheeses.

The Emperor Louis IV of Bavaria fell out of the pope's favor

shortly before being killed on October 1, 1347 while hunting boar. Thus the king himself became what the Latin poets styled *Pabulum Acherontis*: food for Acheron, which was one of the four rivers of the lower region of the dead. The year of the king's death saw the first recorded importation of wheat to England, quite transforming Albion's bakery tradition.

Pope Clement's brilliant, if not unsullied, reign was marred by his failure to end the Hundred Years War, which helps to explain why it lasted 116 years. Clement was intent on relaxing the austerities of his immediate predecessor Benedict XII, whose inability to prevent the start of the Hundred Years War in 1337 is another reason it lasted 116 years. Benedict was a pious reformer, and an innovator in methods of interrogatory torture. It may well be, but this is my speculation: that Clement's attempt to lighten things up in Avignon was influenced by stories passed down about the Christmas feast of King John "Lackland" in 1206 at which 5,006 eggs were served. Such extravagance more than annoyed the barons who produced Magna Carta, which Pope Innocent III condemned as extortion. A similar egg feast was tendered in the same year of 1206 at celebrations for the accession of Qutab-ud-din Aibek, a former slave of Mohammed Ghori, as Sultan of Delhi. The menu scandalized the Jains, those strict followers of an amalgam of Brahmanism and Hinduism, which bans eggs and even bugs from the diet. Classical Roman cults were more Lucullan, hence the expression "ab ovo usque ad mala" (from egg to apples), the equivalent of our soup to nuts.

Back to France, we give thanks that Charles De Gaulle's wife Yvonne stopped their car on August 22, 1962 to buy some frozen chickens; the delay confounded the timing of some terrorists plotting to shoot the great man at a road intersection. Remarkably, this took place on the four hundredth anniversary of the desecration of Clement VI's grave at La Chaise-Dieu by Huguenots who roasted his remains. The grave of the Mozart of cookery, Auguste Escoffier, is in Paris although, let us confess, he did his best work in London during his forty years as a chef at the Reform Club. But if you enter the Parisian temple of kitchen utensils, Battendier's, you will see a picture of the American, Julia Child. Not only can women cook well, they can eat well. As well as the Wagnerian contralto, Ernestine Schumann-Heink, who insisted on eating real food on stage when the scene required it. When the portly diva was asked to turn sideways, she replied that she had no sides. Having made a tremendous debut in Dresden in 1878 as Azecuna in *Il Trovatore*, she performed before Queen Victoria at Windsor Castle. Her autobiography makes one of literature's rare references to the Queen's thick spectacles. She caused a minor sensation by keeping the Queen waiting until she finished her Wiener schnitzel in an ante-chamber. In 1893, she married Paul Schumann, a Hamburger.

Schumann-Heink was born in the same year, 1861, as the dramatic soprano, Nellie Melba. Helen Porter Mitchell took her professional name from her hometown in Australia, which was chartered for William Lamb, the second Viscount Melbourne. Melba toast and Peach Melba were named in Nellie's honor. Six years before singing *Lucia di Lammermoor* at the Metropolitan Opera, she made her debut in Brussels, for which the sprouts are named. In Melba's homeland, as in California and certain other western habitats, the late Bronze Age custom of eating out-of-doors is still practiced, and known as a "barbecue."

Stage heroines yield to the tragic heroine of real life, Marie Antoinette, to whom is imputed the unfeeling line, "Let them eat cake." What she supposedly said was, "Qu'ils mangent de brioche." As brioche is somewhat more available on a limited budget than the fancier gateau, some of the sting is taken from the barb. She probably never said it at all since it was, by Rousseau's attestation a well-known aphorism years before, possibly originating with Madame de Maintenon. It does denote a sensibility higher than the "Let them eat grass" which was uttered by the finance bureaucrat, Joseph Francois Foullon, before a mob hung him from a lamppost in 1789. The propaganda about the cake was spread by sanscullottes who gave Europe fast executions by means of the guillotine, just as modern sanscullottes have given the world fast food. In our period of incivility, not even a return to Avignon could reform things. But it still is nice to reminisce about Pope Clement's 50,000 cakes.

EAST MEETS WEST

ANGLO-SINO-JEWISH CONNECTIONS FORM A TRIANGLE that dismays only those who sniff conspiracies in the Trilateral Commission and fluoridation of water. Ever cautious toward the dangers of launching upon a cultural panorama so eclectic and vast, I offer a few meager examples of ties between these gifted and giving races, like the English broadcaster who gives such useful information about the Hong Kong stock market on the Bloomberg News Radio.

The "No-Popery" excitement in London from June 2 to 8 in 1780, forever stigmatized as the Gordon Riots, sacked Catholic chapels and even attacked the Bank of England. Lord George Gordon (1751–1793), third son of the third duke of Gordon, was a man of extreme commitments, to the point of stoning Papists. He had maintained that the Established Church of England was all that Moses had wanted religion to be, purged of the ritual idiosyncrasies of the Book of Leviticus. When reality knocked loudly enough on the parts of the brain which govern logic, Lord Gordon modified his views but his mind remained a private place where reason was a trespasser. There was a family history of this infrequent collaboration with reality. His forebear, the sixth Earl of Huntly converted from the Church of Rome to the Church of Scotland. Lord Gordon continued to take his own counsel in matters political and spiritual. He libeled Marie Antoinette in 1787 and soon thereafter became a Jew.

The cadet branch of the Lord Gordon's house of Huntly gave mankind Charles George Gordon (1833–1885), whose singular career earned him the tags "Chinese Gordon" and "Gordon Pasha." The general had been hired by the khedive Ismail Pasha to develop the equatorial province of Africa, in the years from 1874 to 1876, during which time the khedive's interest in the Suez Canal was purchased for Britain by Benjamin Disraeli. The prime minister's father, Isaac, in converting from Judaism had taken a course opposite Lord Gordon's, wandering through romantic deserts until he decided that Canterbury was the New Jerusalem. His son writes in his last novel, *Endymion*, that "the Athanasian creed is the most splendid ecclesiastical lyric ever poured forth by the genius of man." Young Disraeli drank so deeply draughts of Anglican waters that he vigorously opposed Gladstone's relaxation of restrictions against Catholics. He also locked horns with Gladstone over General Gordon, whom he supported from mixed motives.

The general so distinguished himself in China that he was made a Mandarin of the First Class in 1865, the same year that the Occident saw him dubbed a Companion of the Bath. As "Chinese Gordon", he returned as governor to the Sudan in 1877 where he confounded the slave trader Suleiman, suppressed slavery, and established British justice. Providence was bountiful in 1877, for in that very year Boris Thomashefsky (1864–1939) arrived in the United States where he began his

life's work of translating Shakespeare's plays into Yiddish. When "Gordon Pasha" fell at the hands of the Mahdi's men in Khartoum on January 26, 1885, Gladstone was shamed and Disraeli posthumously vindicated. Gordon was born in the year Newman wrote "Lead, Kindly Light" and died with a copy of Newman's "Dream of Gerontius" in his pocket. When news of this reached Birmingham, it affected Newman greatly.

Demurral from Jewish belief had different consequences in the parallel lives of Benjamin Disraeli and Karl Marx. In 1883, the apikoros Marx died while Gordon was in Palestine mistakenly thinking he had discovered the real site of Christ's death and resurrection. "Gordon's Calvary" saved Protestant tourists the awkwardness of milling about with Greeks and Armenians and Franciscans in the Church of the Holy Sepulchre. Nineteen years earlier, as Thomashefsky was being born, Marx held his first public meeting to organize the International Working-men's Association.

A random set of threads finally forms an astonishing pattern with the birth in Anhwei of Feng Yu-hsiang in 1880, being both the one hundredth anniversary of the Gordon Riots and the year of Disraeli's resignation as First Lord of the Treasury. Having converted from Confucianism, Feng was known as "The Christian General" in counterpoint to "Chinese Gordon." And a very good general he was, too: a Field Marshall in 1923, in the following year he defeated Wu P'ei-fu and Hsuan T'ung and was largely responsible for the presidency of Tuan Chi-jui. Feng died as the nationhood of Israel was being proclaimed.

Henceforth, the reader should not be able to see an English cottage in some Cotswold dale without imagining pagodas in jasmine gardens and synagogues in busy byways. When Anglo-Saxons and Chinese and Jews can form a fellowship of mind and heart, the mental lights and spiritual powers let loose may give new meaning to the weary word "civilization." Kipling did not think East and West would meet until Judgment Day, but he also said all borders disappear "When two strong men stand face to face, though they come from the ends of the earth!"

THE YANKEES AND WAGNER

IN THE SHAKY SCIENCE OF PROBABILITY, IT IS CONSIDERED bad form to ask, "How can you be sure?" The statistician cannot lose. If he says the odds against winning the state lottery are forty million-to-one (a suspiciously round figure), and someone wins, he can claim he was right. So too with the weatherman who speaks of a 95 percent chance of precipitation and, when the sun comes out, preens that this was the 5 percent.

The odds must be eight trillion-to-one that any two contemporary Major League baseball players, having pitched perfect games, will be found to have attended the same high school. Don Larsen pitched his for the Yankees on an October afternoon in 1956 against the Brooklyn Dodgers, and David Wells pitched his for the Yankees against the Minnesota Twins on a May afternoon in 1998. Both graduated from Point Loma High School in San Diego, Larsen in 1947 and Wells in 1982. In the realm of probabilities, this is more striking than the configuration by which Julius Caesar took 1855 Gauls captive in

55 B.C. for work in the Roman marches, while in 1855 A.D. aluminum sold at $55 per pound.

The Point Loma High School phenomenon has been so publicized that it is too conventional for the connoisseur of co-incidences. Nonetheless, from a rarified purview one may detect an item that was neglected in the hysteria of May 16, 1998 and it is this: the perfect game which gave a halcyon aura to the lives of sports fans on that bucolic day was the thirteenth to have been pitched in the twentieth century. Fascination with the number thirteen has some foundation in the retinue at table on the night Christ was betrayed, but it has intimidated people as diverse as the Vikings and Hindus. The Turks harbor an especially violent dread of thirteen. Irrational fear of the number thirteen is known by everyone today as "triskaideka-phobia." It drives hotels and hospitals to pretend that the thir-teenth floor is the fourteenth. Houses in Paris are not numbered thirteen, notwithstanding the Cartesian common sense of the French. The arithmetic sum of the 265 United States Cavalrymen scalped at Little Big Horn equals the fated number. But Mr. Wells should think thirteen lucky, like the an-cient Mayans who considered it an indicator of special skill and power. Mr. Larsen should also be a triskaidekaphile, particularly since his perfect game was on the thirteen hundredth anniver-sary of the start of the Empress Saimei's great canal in Japan, whose workforce had two platoons of 13,000 each.

Chauncey Depew flashed his famous wit saying, "I am not at all superstitious, but I would not sleep thirteen in a bed on a Friday night." But if he was innocent of triskaidekaphobia, we must call it mere coincidence that he quit the Senate in 1911 after serving twelve years. Charles Stewart Parnell so dreaded

thirteen that he once introduced into a Land Bill a fourteenth clause he had opposed in principle. His rationality on such matters was not beyond question; he also thought the color green was accursed, which was an inconvenient superstition for a man who in his years was unofficially the uncrowned king of Ireland. Depew was elected to the United States Senate thirteen years after Gladstone indicated support of Parnell's measure for Irish home-rule.

For the dark and driven Richard Wagner, thirteen had mixed connotations. His own name has thirteen letters and he was born in 1813, the digital sum of which is thirteen, and he died seventy years later on February 13. His mentor Liszt, who first met him on September 13 in 1841, visited him on October 13, 1854 in Switzerland where Wagner had fled from Dresden on May 13, 1849, and where he was exiled for thirteen years. Wagner finished *The Flying Dutchman* on a September 13, premiered *Tannhauser* on a March 13 and the *Ring of the Nibelun-*

gen on an August 13. With a one-hour intermission, the Ring Cycle lasts thirteen hours. Wagner first heard *Lohengrin* performed thirteen years after its completion, wrote thirteen stage works, was married to Cosima for thirteen years and died thirteen months after finishing *Parsifal* on May 13, 1882.

This wizard of Bayreuth went dotty. The feel of coarse fabric was intolerable, so he only wore silks and satins and even covered his ceiling in Munich with silk; the corners of his rooms were rounded off because he could not abide acute angles. I know I open myself to charges of bias, because I do not like that master of Nazi elevator music. Anyone who enjoys the entire Ring Cycle should be denied the right to bear arms. But even I cannot claim that he was more Turk than Mayan when it came to the number thirteen.

Our nation was born of thirteen colonies, and the New York Exposition of 1853 covered thirteen acres. Pope Leo XIII was the greatest Leo since the first one and issued his greatest encyclical *Rerum novarum* in the thirteenth year of his pontificate. In 13 A.D. Drusus began his felicitous governance of Batavia. The year 1300 marked the acme of human civilization (if we cast a blind eye to the antics of Alexander III in Hungary) and each subsequent century has only added a splinter to the twisting spiral of decay.

Not one of America's autochthonous sports commentators alluded to any of the above on May 16, 1998. They probably were also ignorant of the famous wager of the uncanonized patron of probability science: Pascal said that, given the odds, any sensible man should bet on eternal life. Had he lived today, great Pascal would not have failed to remark the digital sum of the 127 feet 3 inches regulation diagonal distance between first and third bases.

KEEPING TIME

THE AZTECS COULD TELL TIME ON A MEGA-SCALE, BEING keen on sun dials and calendars. If there was not some contact with the East, we are confronted with a mega-coincidence: four of the twelve animal symbols in the Mongolian zodiac calendar are identical with those used by the Aztecs, and three others differ only as the respective species differ in the two parts of the world.

The Aztecs calculated the arrival of their white god, Quetzalcoatl. Although Hernando Cortes had only 600 Spanish troops and sixteen horses, and the capital city Tenochtitlan had 350,000 inhabitants, the Aztecs easily fell to him because his arrival was congruent with many of their prophecies. In 1510, Montezuma's sister, Papantzin, had described the invasion in detail from a dream. The arrival of Cortes at Montezuma's citadel ten years later was in the climactic year of a 52-year cycle according to the Aztec configuration. The Mayan system of similar cycles was so precise that it could pinpoint any date within a range of 370,000 years. Montezuma's priests were persuaded that the Spaniards were harbingers of the apocalyptic fall of the Fifth and Last Sun. The Spaniards' use of horses and shooting sticks further matched the Aztec prophecies, and Montezuma's twenty-eight-year reign collapsed largely as a result of his own conviction that this was fate. Cortes was likewise impressed by the date of his confrontation with Montezuma: Good Friday.

By this time, the Julian Calendar instituted by Julius Caesar in 46 B.C. was off the earth's solar cycle by ten days. Sensitive souls felt the discrepancy in their very bones. Pope Gregory XIII's astronomers gave us his improvement, certified at the Villa Mondragone near Frascati, and by decree of the Bull "Inter Gravissimas" the fifth of October became the fifteenth in 1582. St. Teresa of Avila died in Alba de Tormes three hours before midnight as the new calendar went into effect so, through no fault of her own, the saint died ten days apart.

It has long been thought fortuitous that Shakespeare, whose Henry V enjoined the cry "God for Harry! England and Saint George!", was born, as far as can be determined, on St. George's Day, April 23, in 1564. Only pedants in the Oxford Alumni Association of New York persist in holding an annual wine and cheese birthday party for him on April 22. Beyond mere wonder is this: Shakespeare also died on April 23, in 1616. And far beyond mere wonder is the death of Cervantes, the "Spanish Shakespeare" on the same day. One restrains oneself from the use of an exclamation point. Note that we must say the same "day" and not the same date. Shakespeare's England was still on the Julian calendar. The same year saw the birth of Andreas Gryphius, the "German Shakespeare", who died on the centenary of the English Shakespeare's birth.

Pope Gregory's calendar was more successful than some of his other projects: an Irish invasion of England, the assassina-

tion of Elizabeth I, a celebration of the St. Bartholomew's Day Massacre, and the mass conversion of Sweden and Russia. England did not adopt the popish Gregorian calendar until 1752 under the "Chesterfield Act." Political and religious propaganda caused riots by mobs persuaded that the Pope of Rome had taken eleven days out of their lives, for by then another day had been added to the disparity. "Give us back our eleven days!" was their cry, and it is vividly depicted in an engraving by Hogarth. London was in disarray, the commons of Liverpool were disordered beyond the usual, and several rioters in Bristol were actually killed in the *turba calendae*. Thus the Church's patronage of science was trashed by creatures of the Enlightenment. Such stupidity will always mark the bigot. As Vice President Gore has said, "A leopard never changes his stripes." Other Protestant lands succumbed earlier. In 1688 William of

Orange left Holland on November 11 and arrived in England on November 5. Although the Stroganovs began the conquest of Siberia in the first year of the Gregorian reform, Russia did not change until 1918.

Rabbi Emil Hirsch was born in Luxembourg and moved to Chicago in 1866, where he used the Hebrew and Gregorian calendars and caused a flap as the first Reformed rabbi to move Sabbath services from Saturday to Sunday, just when Rachel D. Preston persuaded the Seventh-Day Adventists to switch the Sabbath from Sunday to Saturday. Hirsh arrived in Chicago, curiously enough, on the one hundredth anniversary of the birth of Domingo Badia y Leblich who mastered the Muslim calendar and became the first Christian known to have visited Mecca.

Pope Gregory's calendar, with its system of Leap Years, should last for at least another thousand years. You can tell what day of the week any day will fall on by a simple method: increase by 1/4 the number formed by the last two digits of the year in question, add 2 if this is 18 (minus fractions), 0 if this is 19, and 6 if this is 20. To this sum, add 1 if the month is January or October, 2 if May, 3 if August, 4 if February or March or November, 5 if June, 6 if September or December, 0 if April or July. If it is a Leap Year, add 6 for January and 3 for February. Then add the day of the month and divide by 7. The remainder indicates the day of the week, and if there is no remainder the answer is Saturday. The same Pope Gregory also helped to streamline the Vatican government.

FOR WHOM
THE BELL TOLLS

AS PART OF ITS GAME PLAN FOR THE THIRD MILLEN-
nium, the United States Conference of Catholic Bishops has
sanctioned cremation. Previous church practice had been
against this, except in emergency situations such as the Spanish
Inquisition. The bishops predict an increase in the number of
dead people. With greater specificity, the Scottish poet Thomas
of Erceldoune (c.1220–1297) predicted the death of King
Alexander III (d.1286) and the Battle of Bannockburn (1314).
The French physician and astrologer and crypto-Lutheran
Michel de Notredame (1503–1566) was on the mark when he
said Henry II would die in 1555. The Oxford clergyman Robert
Burton (1577–1640) played medic in his potpourri of learning,
The Anatomy of Melancholy, and dated his own death ten years
before the melancholy event. If it can be argued that the coincidence was psychosomatic, it must also be admitted that dying
is a flamboyant way of being correct.

Wedged between the generations of Alexander III and
Henry II is the matter of Timur Lenk's tomb. We know this ra-

pacious descendant of Genghis Khan as Tamerlane, as we know
Michel de Notredame as Nostradamus. It is tempting to specu-
late whether Tamerlane drew on the mysticism of heretical
Christians. Some of the family of Genghis Khan, including his
grandson Hulagu, had been converted by Nestorian missionaries among the Tartar Onguts and Vighurs north of the Yellow
River. There even was a Nestorian bishop in Beijing when it
was called Cambaluc. And all this because the Emperor Li-
Shih-Min admitted the Nestorians into China sixty-three years
before Pope Sergius baptized the Wessex king Caedwalla. The
year 63 happens to be the traditional year of St. Paul's release
from house arrest in Rome. Anyway, having conquered Persia,
Central Asia and breathtaking stretches of Russia, India and
Asia Minor, Tamerlane chose to be buried near his birthplace
in Samarkand of Uzbekistan. The fatal year was 1405. He ordered the epitaph: "If I should be exhumed, the worst of all
wars will overwhelm this land." At 5 a.m. on June 22, 1941,
Soviet scientists uncovered Tamerlane's remains. At the same
hour, the German army crossed the Russian border.

In all its chill and foreboding, that surpasses the coincidence of October 4, 1981, the two hundredth anniversary of Rome's *ex post facto* condemnation of Nostradamus. It is actually a multiple coincidence, for on that notable bicentenary, the body of Lee Harvey Oswald was exhumed, fifty years to the hour after Clyde Pangborn and Hugh Herndon arrived in Wenatchee, Washington from Japan in the first non-stop flight across the Pacific Ocean. Speaking of Japan, many Asians consider it good fortune to be a twin and the best of fortunes to die on one's birthday. It is fitting that Michael Vaillancourt Aris, Oxford's leading authority on Tibetan and Himalayan studies and husband of Nobel Peace Prize winner Daw Aung San Suu Kyi, was born along with his brother Anthony on March 27, 1946 and died on March 27, 1999.

That exotic drawing room spiritualist Count Louis Hamon, who went by the name of Cheiro, was taken more than half-seriously by some, while others thought him at best amusing. It is not certain that Napoleon III consulted this Hamon like some latter-day Ahasuerus, although the emperor reportedly persuaded Queen Victoria to partake of a séance in Osborne House. In 1894, fifteen years after Napoleon's son, the Prince Imperial, was killed in a Zulu ambush while fighting in the British army, Count Hamon told Lord Kitchener, then a forty-four-year-old sirdar of the Egyptian army: "I can see nothing but success and honors for you in the next two decades. You will become one of the most illustrious men in the land. But after that, your life is at great risk. I see a disaster at sea taking place in your sixty-sixth year." In 1916, aged sixty-six, Kitchener drowned in the sinking of the "Hampshire" off the coast of Orkney. As the ship sank, a hatchment in the home of Count Hamon broke in two. Churchill had berated Kitchener for violating the sacred shrine of the Mahdi in the Sudan. The Mahdi's tomb had a warning: "He who desecrates the graves of religious leaders will perish through water floods and the place of his death will never be known."

How can one resist thoughts of a "curse" without some supernal bondage to empirical principles? Take "King Tut's Curse." The fifth earl of Carnarvon, George Edward Stanhope Molyneux Herbert funded and worked with Howard Carter in excavating tombs of the XIIth and XVIIIth dynasties, exhuming the remains of Tutankhamen from their glittering sarcophagus. When the earl died from an infection in 1923, his pet terrier bitch stood on her hind legs, howled and collapsed dead. Even allowing for the histrionics which are characteristic of many terriers, this behavior astonished sanguine observers. As the earl and his terrier died, all the electric lights in Cairo failed. The highly regarded Cairo Electric Board was never able to account for the blackout.

Old people do not need a soothsayer to hear time's sure scythe. Two of America's most important candy barons died at great ages in 1999 to no one's surprise: the one hundred-year-old inventor of Bonomo's Turkish Taffy, and the ninety-five-year-old inventor of the M & M chocolates and the Mars Bar. Eyebrows do rise at the coincidence of their deaths. Five years apart in age, they died five days apart and both in Florida: Victor Bonomo on June 26 and Forrest Mars on July 1. Bonomo's father Albert, a Sephardic Jew, started making candy in Coney Island on the six hundredth anniversary of the death of Thomas of Erceldoune.

Then there are clocks. The clock over the entrance to Tiffany's stopped on April 15, 1865 at 7:22 a.m., the moment

Lincoln stopped. The clock at Sandringham in the bedroom of King George VI did the same during the night of February 5, 1952, when the king died of a coronary thrombosis. But Shakespeare's line in *King John* still ticks on: "Old Time the clock-setter, that bald sexton, Time." And so sings on the parlor song about the grandfather's clock that "stopped short, never to go again when the old man died."

Having pursued a difficult subject with delicacy, I must refrain from cliché and not remind the reader of what John Donne said about the tolling bell. Like the curious incident of Sherlock Holmes's dog that did not bark, more telling is the bell that will not toll.

THE MADNESS
OF MANY

YOUR SCRIVENER WRITES THESE WORDS WITH CAUTION,
for he is well aware of the power of coincidences to drive men
mad. When someone mistakenly attributes a coincidence to
enigmatic causes, the mind can reel right off the edge. I think
of that woman who went bonkers ever so briefly when she
blamed the New York City blackout of 1965 on her electric
iron. Every freshman knows from the most cursory reading of
the etiology of psychosis that there are varieties of mental de-
lapidation, and not all are caused by mistaken causality. Nor
are all clinically insane people unproductive. While confined
to institutions for the bewildered, Christopher Smart
(1722–1771) wrote hymns, Richard Dadd (1817–1887) painted
fairies, and Ezra Pound (1885–1972) edited his dithyrambs on
Mussolini. Smart kept up his friendship with Thomas Gray and
Samuel Johnson during his mental occlusion, penning from his
cell the "Song to David" with such rhymed couplets as "Glorious the thunder's roar . . . Glorious the martyr's gore." Dadd
went to Bedlam after killing his own dad in a crazed state when

he thought that he was being pursued by the Egyptian god Osiris. As for Pound, his political views were less measured than his verse. He was an inmate of St. Elizabeth's Hospital in Washington, D.C., where an insane asylum is like a sandbox in the Sahara Desert.

Sometimes irreason seems positively reasonable. I have elsewhere told the story of Sir Thomas Styles of the First Foot Guards who was driven to distraction by fleas in the Peninsular War. Many of us would have reacted the same way. A frayed mental fabric often seems woven in genetic patterns. Such may have been so of Mary Todd Lincoln who was behaving oddly long before her confinement in 1875. Just as strange as her behavior is the fact that she was born six years after the author of nonsense rhymes, Edward Lear (1812–1888), and died six years before him. The name Nasticreechia Krorluppia appeared in Lear's Nonsense Botany in 1870, the year Congress granted Mrs. Lincoln a pension.

Nor does everyone, thankfully, respond the same way to coincidences. Let me cite traffic as a case in point. As early as

1806 Napoleon furiously had demanded the removal of Ercole Cardinal Consalvi (1757–1824), but he grudgingly respected the Papal Secretary of State's character. Returning to Italy from Beziers, Consalvi's coach rolled through Frejus at the moment Napoleon's coach passed in the opposite direction on the way to his first exile in Elba. Their eyes met and His Majesty muttered of His Eminence, who was a deacon: "There, that man who would never become a priest, is a better priest than them all." So Napoleon kept his cool and was even edified by the phenomenal coincidence. On the other hand, Lady Caroline Lamb (1785–1828) was absolutely uncool in traffic. The novelist had a nine-month love affair with Lord Byron while she was married to Lord Melbourne. In 1824, she happened upon a funeral procession passing along the road and, learning that it was Byron's, she immediately went berserk. The Duchess of Devonshire behaved almost as extravagantly at Cardinal Consalvi's wake in the Palazzo Farnese. Madame Recamier, famously accustomed to lying on the sofa named for herself, was standing by and caught the Duchess as she fainted at the catafalque and took her back to the Palazzo Spada. Within two months, the Duchess was dead, succumbing in Rome on the actual day that Henry Clay delivered in Congress his famous speech in favor of protective tariffs.

A Berlin carpenter named Joseph Friederick (1790–1873) built a miniature ivory model of the Church of St. Nicholas in Potsdam. A crack appeared in one of the miniature columns and, a few weeks later, an identical crack appeared in the corresponding spot in the real church. Friederick inspected this and became unhinged, never to become quite whole again.

There have always been oddities among the religious. Clinical psychologists often apply to them the term "nut." Like Herostratus, who set fire to the fourth temple of Diana in Ephesus in 356 B.C., on what turned out to be coincidentally the traditional birth date of Alexander the Great. Some are only crazy like foxes: Father Divine, for example, who claimed to have killed a civil judge by the power of prayer. Others are plain out looney. Ludowick Muggleton comes to mind. In England in 1651, he and his cousin John Reeves capitalized on the excitement surrounding the Navigation Act mandating the seizure of Dutch vessels, to advertise themselves as the "two witnesses" of Revelation 11: 3–6. They promised to prophesy for 1,260 days. When they finished, nothing happened, unless you want to count the Tartar invasion of Poland. With such fragile issue, the Muggletonians died out.

Lenin died when the Anglican Bishop of Birmingham publicly condemned bridge-playing as a wasteful activity. It is most improbable that Lenin died in reaction to the condemnation. It seems quite evident that the bishop, not heedless of Lenin's ill health, misread the significance of the moment. We should say the bishop was not mad, but only lacked a sense of proportion.

Many of the above may have been fanatics rather than madmen. Mr. Dooley said a fanatic is one who thinks God would agree with him if He had all the facts. The fanatic has no sense of humor because humor requires perception of imbalance. The madman may have a sense of humor but it is backwards; it perceives balance and laughs at that. Not to laugh at coincidences is prescription for weeping at coincidences, and that way lies endless madness. The one kind of humor that always gets this right is literally graceful. A mad world calls it madness, but in small sane pockets of that world it is called sanctity.

BEFORE INCUNABULA

Some essays write themselves and this is one of them. In 1996 the philanthropist George W. Mallinckrodt gave a substantial gift to the Bodleian Library of Oxford University to preserve its vast collection of incunabula. When the gift was announced, Mr. Mallinckrodt said it was "a happy coincidence that one of my ancestors, the Canon of Munster Cathedral, Bernhard von Mallinckrodt, was the first to use the word incunabula about books when, back in 1640, he wrote his pioneering work on the invention of printing." The benefaction most certainly would have gratified and intrigued Sir Thomas Bodley, who enjoyed collecting manuscripts both in his native land and as minister to the Hague from 1589 to 1596.

If there is one subject more fascinating than incunabula, it is what we might call pre-incunabula, with all due respect to Canon von Mallinckrodt. And for the average householder, even more beguiling than a mediaeval Christian manuscript is a mediaeval Islamic manuscript whose flowing calligraphy is literally what is meant by "arabesque." A *très riche* French Book of Hours is not comparable because its glory is in the painting, not in the letters; perhaps only the Celtic gospel pages can challenge the Arab script. A scholar is working on the first volume of *A New Catalogue of Islamic Arabic Manuscripts in the Bodleian Library*. This is particularly concerned with medieval manuscripts, since the last time Islamic Arabic manuscripts of that period were catalogued in Latin by the Bodleian was in 1835.

Of special interest is the coincidence of two such specimens, one of which has been in the Bodleian for 300 years and the other for 200 years. Both are supposedly by the same scribe and both were completed on a date which, on the Christian calendar, is August 22, 1188. The mind reels at this: not only does each manuscript consist of 193 folios, or 386 pages, numerically matching the year B.C. when the Corinth-Argos federation was dissolved, but the Arab scribe was finishing his arduous work exactly as Pope Clement III was declaring the Scottish bishops independent of the Archbishops of Canterbury and York. As that anonymous didact must have been wearily laying down his pen, Archbishops Baldwin and Giraldus Cambrensis were trying to excite the sullen Welsh under Prince Dafydd ab Owain Gwynedd to join the Third Crusade, partly in response to the Battle of Hattin the year before, which had opened Jerusalem to the Arabs. News of Hattin may have reached the scribe as his red and black inks were drying, the city of Stockholm was being founded, and the Kakatiyas of Warangal were establishing themselves in the Indian ascendancy of the Rajput states. Four short years later, the head of the Minamoto clan, Yoritomo, would become Sei-i-tai Shogun (Barbarian Subjugating Commander-in-Chief) in Kamakura. The imagination is taxed by another stunning circumstance: in the year of Canon von Mallinckrodt's treatise on incunabula, a large embassage of

Portuguese from Macao would be beheaded by the third Toku-
gawa Shogun, a distant successor of Yoritomo.

Thus two obscure sets of Islamic folios expose a vast inter-
cultural horizon. This should not be surprising if we realize that
an astonishing triad of the most distinguished satirical poets in
Iraqi history were contemporaries in the Ommiad period: Jarir
(d.727) who was a Christian, and the Muslims, al-Akhtal
(ca.640–710) and al-Farazdaq (ca.640–732). They were all of
an age before religious feelings hardened and sartirical verse became more acerbic.

The folios of 1188 have a charm typical of so many Arabic manuscripts inscribed with such poetic appeals as "Oh, Buttercup!" This exclamation (Ya Kabiraj) appears because buttercups were considered a useful repellent against insects attracted to the fish-glue, starch, and honey used in the binding of folios. The Ayyubid rulers could not have anticipated the "poor little Buttercup" that all the world now knows, but she appeared in the first performance of "H.M.S. Pinafore" on the 700th anniversary of the apex of their power in Egypt.

For pre-incunabulists the drama now reaches fever pitch. The folios of 1188 were submitted to the Scanning Proton Microprobe Unit of the Oxford Nuclear Physics Laboratory in 1994. Both sets of folios were almost photographically identical—including every line and shading and shake of the pen—but the laboratory analysis could not account for this, nor did it offer a hypothesis to explain why all that was written in red ink in one set is absent from the other. Six years earlier, this Oxford laboratory was one of three which stirred controversy by carbon dating the Shroud of Turin to sometime between 1260 and 1390.

The virtual identity of the two folios remains what experts call an "unsolvable conundrum." Further research on the Islamic manuscripts may shed light on the Shroud, and vice versa. One lesson from the romance of pre-incunabula is plain: it is unscientific to pass off a forgery as a coincidence or a coincidence as forgery. On this, one likes to think, the diverse movers and shakers of 1188 would agree, including a pope, a maharajah, and a shogun.

THE SAVAGE BREAST SOOTHED

As MUSIC IS BY A UNIVERSAL CONSENT OF PHILOSOPHY the highest of arts, it can be counted on to have the most inspiring effect on the intellect and will. So phenomenal a power, able to smooth the stern brow and sooth the savage breast, must have other influences too. The art of the gods at their lyres may actually cause bewilderment, especially when it becomes entangled in a morass of inexplicable coincidences.

For starters, there is the example of national anthems. It is an open secret that the Austrian anthem was based by Haydn on the Croatian song, "Vjutro rano se ja vstanem." That is merely a curiosity and no odder than taking "The Star Spangled Banner" from an English drinking song. More than only curious is this: Julia Ward Howe, author of what may be unofficially our second national anthem, "The Battle Hymn of the Republic", died in the same year (1910) as Bjornstjerne Bjornson, author of the Norwegian national anthem "Ja, Vi Elsker Dette Landet."

Again, it may be nothing more than a curiosity that neither

Richard Wagner nor Hector Berlioz could play the piano, so both composed their works on the guitar. But while the operettist Jeanette MacDonald sang a less complex repertoire, she left the musical world a poignant circumstance long to be pondered, dying on a stage in Detroit on January 24, 1965 as she was singing her signature song "Ciribiribin." In a different milieu, in 1230, Walther von der Vogelweide, the Rudy Vallee of Swabia, sang his last song as a five-year-old Thomas Aquinas was entering Monte Cassino.

Surpassing odd is the extraordinary length of Donald J. Grout's *Short History of Opera*, nearly twice the size of his whole *History of Western Music*. Other oddities pile up if you listen for them with a sharp enough ear and sense of timing. Chaucer's prologue to his *Canterbury Tales* can be sung to the tune of "Glow Little Glow-Worm" and all the published poems of Emily Dickinson can be sung to the tune of "The Yellow Rose of Texas."

I should be glad to let items like that pass. They harm none and take the butter off no man's bread. There is a coincidence that cannot be ignored or passed off as simply odd, however, and it will palpitate until the last note is sung by the last human voice: Johann Sebastian Bach was born in Eisenach, George Frederic Handel was born in Halle, and Domenico Scarlatti was born in Naples, all in 1685. Both Handel and Scarlatti were twenty-four years old when they participated in a Roman musical competition presided over by Cardinal Ottoboni. Bach and Handel had the same oculist (Handel going completely blind after submitting to the man's scalpel) and Handel and Scarlatti had weight problems, although Scarlatti's obesity was greater to the extent that he had difficulty crossing

his hands at the keyboard of a harpsichord. As a resident of London's Mayfair, Handel lived at 25 Brook Street. In 1970 the rock star Jimi Hendrix lived in the house next door. The Handel House Trust marked the coincidence by designating a room to commemorate Hendrix as part of a planned Handel museum.

The Italians have a saying, "E meglio cader dalle finistre che del tetto", the deeper sense of which is obscure though it basically means that it is better to fall out of windows than off a roof. The phrase must be from a period after Tasso's golden age of aphorisms. I should think that, applied to music, it could mean that it would be better to be fat or even blind than deaf.

Which reminds us: Johann Nepomuk Maelzel died on an American brig, the "Otis", sailing to the West Indies when Emily Dickinson was only eight years old. That German mechanical marvel is perhaps best celebrated for having invented the metronome named for him, but we invoke his spectre here because he designed Ludwig van Beethoven's ear trumpet.

Soon and sadly enough, certainly by 1819, Beethoven's hearing degenerated beyond any aid Maelzel could invent. Evelyn Waugh, having published *Vile Bodies* on the centenary of Emily Dickinson's birth, began to affect an ear trumpet which he did not need, in order to attract attention. Beethoven would not have been amused. Obesity, as we have observed, poses some difficulties for musicians, and so does blindness, though the latter also can stimulate the musical sense. But deafness in a musician is high tragedy, and for a composer to lose his hearing would be like a scholar losing his mind or a bishop losing his voice.

Winding up this musical interlude is a circumstance both curious and coincidental. On the centenary of the Metropolitan Opera, October 22, 1984, an intruder crashed the gates of the Augusta National Golf Course and took seven hostages as President Reagan was teeing off. It was also the fifteenth anniversary of the discovery of the famous cache of virginal and lute books in Forfarshire, Scotland, the birthplace of golf.

The decline of music in our day to a new and awful corybanticism, should concern us all. Consolation is rare, but if it is to be found, it will be by pressing to our nation's savage breast the considerations above which I have brought before the attention of what one hopes is a not inattentive audience, to the end that they might become more lyrical than perplexed.

NOBLE THOUGHTS

ALTHOUGH PERSIAN AND ENGLISH SHARE NO ETYMOLOG-
ical roots, the words "bad" and "soup" mean the same in both.
Thus an American might say to an Iranian chef, "bad soup" and
be perfectly understood. This should alert us to another coincidence involving speakers of those two tongues. During World
War II Prince Hamid Qajar, who died in 1988, fought in the
British Royal Navy under the pseudonym David Drummond,
serving on H.M.S. Duke of York at the Battle of North Cape.
One evening, the Ukrainian pianist, Lev Pouishnov, stayed on
board that vessel during a concert visit to Scapa Flow. After
dinner in the wardroom, Pouishnov showed the officers his
gold cigarette case with ingeniously concealed hinges. Lieutenant "Drummond" produced an identical case from his own
pocket, whereupon Pouishnov dropped to his knee and kissed
the lieutenant's hand. The pianist later confided to a friend:
"That is the heir to the throne of Persia. His father gave me my
cigarette case years ago after a concert."

Tobacco figures in another royal coincidence. Augustin Fer-
nández Muñoz was the son of a tobacconist, but left that trade
to become a royal guard. During an afternoon drive in 1833,

Maria Cristina, Queen Regent of Spain as mother of King Fernando III, had a nose-bleed. The young corporal, one of her escorts, gave her a handkerchief. Several months later, the same corporal was once again in attendance when the royal carriage skidded off the road in the Guadarrama mountains, and once again he offered the Queen a handkerchief. Soon they secretly married and he was made a Grandee of the First Order and Duke of Riansares. In a strange juxtaposition, the Swiss Canton of Basel was divided in two the same year these two were joined together.

In 1919, Nancy Langhorne Astor, Virginia tobacco and land heiress in addition to what she acquired by marriages to Robert Gould Shaw and Waldorf Astor, became the first woman to take a seat in the House of Commons, replacing her husband when he became the second Viscount Astor and entered the House of Lords. In the same year that Lady Astor began her stormy political career, Princess Ayesha, daughter of the Maharaja of Cooch Behar, was born in India, where Nancy Astor's brother-in-law had been aide-de-camp to the Viceroy until 1914. When Ayesha attained the diadem of Jaipur, she became the first Maharani to sit in Parliament. Named for Mohammed's chief wife, the daughter of abu-Bakr, her religion required that she eschew tobacco products.

Here the tobacco connection with nobility fades, but the royal coincidences perdure. In 1961 Hope Cooke of the United States accepted the proposal of marriage of the Maharaj-Prince Sikkim Palden Thondup Namgyal, who became King of Sikkim in 1963, the same year that Queen Margrethe of Denmark first met her future husband, Count Henri de Laborde de Montpezat. And on the 125th anniversary of the Australian Parliament in 1975, the exiled King Leka I of Albania fell in love with Susan Cullen-Ward, daughter of an Australian sheep farmer.

A more elevated coincidence attaches to St. Elizabeth of Hungary (1207–1231) and St. Elizabeth of Portugal (1271–1336), for the saints were queens of their respective countries, matched each other in Franciscan solicitude for the poor, and were related: the Hungarian was a great-aunt of the Portuguese. Not to mention that they had the same names. Neither smoked.

Far different in spiritual expression was King George I of England who spoke no English. In conversation with his Prime Minister, Robert Walpole, who spoke no German, he spoke Latin, although both opposed the Church of Rome. King George, like most of the Hanoverians, enjoyed a bit of angling, which gives a nice touch to the fact that a collateral descendant, James Ogilvy, son of HRH the Princess Alexandra, was attacked by a shark without incident in Bermuda in November, 1987. Shortly thereafter, a sea gull dropped a rubber fish into his golf cart. This certainly was as strange as the famous incident of the eagle dropping a tortoise on the head of Aeschylus. Coming right on the heels of the shark attack, it was even stranger.

It is said that King Edward VII spoke with something of a German accent, which is not surprising given his unpleasant early home life. At the height of Hanoverian influence, in 1768 to be exact, in a quiet corner of an Essex garden an Auricula plant produced 133 blooms. Widely remarked then by horticulturists, we remember the plant now for a different reason: the sum of 1768 and 133 is the year of Edward's accession. Queen Alexandra, who loathed Germans almost to the point of irreason because of her Danish blood and experience, admired and cultivated the Auricula, apparently unaware of the phenomenon of 1768. She also permitted her husband one last cigar as he was dying in 1910, thus bringing our reverie full circle. In the final reckoning, even crowns are as ephemeral as rings of smoke. At least royal governors are spectacles more enjoyable than uncrowned heads of state who forbid their supposedly free fellow citizens to smoke at all. And this is so notwithstanding the warning of the thespian Brooke Shields: "Smoking kills. If you're killed, you've lost a very important part of your life."

A NATION MOURNS

ADOLF FREDERICK V, GRAND DUKE OF MECKLENBURG-Strelitz, was born during the presidency of James Knox Polk who was born in Mecklenburg County, North Carolina. We might focus on mighty Polk's birth, as that *partum* from his mother's womb coincided with the Third Partition of Poland. A more dour eye would rather focus on his death, simultaneous with that of King William II of Holland. Optimists, like myself, prefer to think of births attached to the presidency, although I have only known one person actually born in the White House and he was a clergyman, Francis B. Sayre, grandson of Wilson. The increased number of mind-altering synthetic palliatives on the market may increase the ranks of optimists. There will always be pessimists, however, and pessimists are more aware of obsequies.

On a macabre chart, all U.S. presidents elected at twenty year intervals from 1840 to 1960 died in office. The first, Harrison died of pneumonia after one month in office, having caught a chill at his inauguration. The interval between the Treaty of Aix la Chapelle in 1748 (on the centenary of which the Grand Duke of Mecklenburg-Strelitz was born) and the assassination of McKinley in 1901 is identical to the interval between Harrison's golden day at Tippecanoe in 1811 and the death of the vaudeville star Eddie Cantor in 1964.

As one might expect, more presidents died in retirement than in office. Only in a moral sense have some seemed to have died before entering office, and these should not becloud the pantheon of true heroes. A tremendous civil mysticism surrounds the deaths of Thomas Jefferson and John Adams on the fiftieth anniversary of July 4, 1776. It was an event so redolent of ancient auguries that we should just recognize that it happened and trust that it was a portentous benediction from the Supreme Governor. James Monroe died five years later, also on Independence Day. James Madison would have done the same another five years later, but he refused his physicians' offer of stimulants and died instead on June 28. This is matched only by King William IV dying in 1837 on "Waterloo Day", June 18, the anniversary of the battle. Vaguer than usual as he expired, nonetheless he was fully aware of what day it was and died clutching a French banner captured on the field of victory. His queen, Adelaide of Saxe-Meiningen, knelt by the bedside and then got up and died twelve years later in the same year as Dolley Madison, occasioning an elegant panegyric by the manic-depressive preacher of Brighton, Frederick William Robertson. Field Marshall Montgomery was born on the fiftieth anniversary of King William's death. But that is an optimistic intrusion on our pessimistic panorama. Better to recall Queen Mary and Cardinal Pole dying of unrelated causes on November 15, 1558.

"When he went, the power and the glory of the presidency went with him." So mourned Coolidge on the death of his son and namesake in 1924, which was the 500th anniversary of the death of the venerated heretic John Zizka in Bohemia—a

wrenching moment for the not habitually ebullient Hussites. The presidents of both sides in the Civil War lost young sons during their administrations. Lincoln's son William Wallace ("Willie") died in the White House from typhus on February 12, 1862 at the age of twelve. On April 30, 1864, the five-year-old Joseph ("Joe") Davis died in a fall from the veranda of the Confederate presidential mansion.

More haunting in retrospect is the rescue of Willie's brother, Robert Todd in 1864. As the young man leaned over the edge of a Pennsylvania Railroad platform in Jersey City, the press of the crowd caused him to stumble onto the tracks as a locomotive approached. He was pulled to safety by the firm hand of the actor Edwin Booth, brother of the future assassin of Robert's father. Robert became Ambassador to Great Britain and, overcoming any fear of locomotives, president of the Pullman Company from 1897 to 1911, the centenary of the Battle of Tippecanoe. Having attended his own father's deathbed, he was present at the assassinations of Garfield in 1881 and William McKinley in 1901. For official invitations to presidential functions thereafter, a prudent chief of protocol would have switched him to the "B" list.

Theodore, the good Roosevelt, indulged no superstitions of that sort, painfully acquainted though he was with the Grim Reaper. In New York City on St. Valentine's Day in 1884, his mother Martha died from typhus at 3:00 a.m. and his wife Alice died in childbirth from complications caused by Bright's disease at 2:11 p.m.

On the same day President Kennedy was shot in 1963, C. S. Lewis and Aldous Huxley died more peacefully, though their deaths got lost in the torrent of political publicity. A century or so from the perspective may change, for monitoring kingdoms is not the way to measure true power and glory.

It has become an automatic convention in conversation today to refer to any fraudulent oracle as a Paphlagonian. This goes back to Alexander the Paphlagonian, an imposter of the second century. President Lincoln, who was no Paphlagonian, did seem to have some genuine foreboding, with his dreams about the ship in a storm. On the day of his assassination he signed an act creating the Secret Service. And all who know salvation history know the dream Pontius Pilate's wife dreamed. She may have thought it coincidental that when she awoke the sky started to die. But Judea was a backwater far from Rome. Imperial attention at the time noted only one death of importance, the execution of Germanicus's son Drusus.

DETACHMENT

To investigate the quack theory of animal magne-
tism, a hypothesis of Franz Mesmer (1743–1815) for whom Mes-
merism is named, King Louis XVI appointed a committee which
included Benjamin Franklin (1706–1790) for whom the Franklin
stove is named, and Joseph Guillotin (1738–1814) for whom the
guillotine is named. The king's own decapitation on that swift
and sanguineous machine was, as an American high school text-
book has it, fatal. The three persons to whom the exhumer Mr.
Cox showed Oliver Cromwell's desiccated head, suffered abrupt
deaths. Heads have always been important, although in many in-
stances their value has been symbolic. Thus in 1988 the New
Zealand government got an injunction to stop Bonhams, the
London auction house, from selling the preserved head of a Maori
warrior; and in 1998 a New York dealer was fined $29,000 for sell-
ing Seminole and Peoria Indian skulls. New Zealand's action took
place coincidentally on the 150th anniversary of Sir James
Brooke's embarkation to the Malay Archipelago where, as Raja of
Sarawak, he would unsuccessfully prohibit headhunting.

The head is not the only detachable part of the body. As
Washington Irving (1783–1859) told the tale of a headless

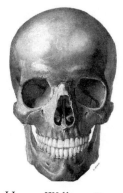

horseman in *The Legend of Sleepy Hollow*, it is apposite that Sir Paulus Irving (1751–1821) was captured in 1777 at Saratoga, where Benedict Arnold was wounded on October 7 in a leg, the knee of which had previously been shot at Quebec. A fulsome agitator against the Americans was the second Earl of Dartmouth (1731–1801) whose family name was Legge. The first Marquis of Anglesey, Henry William Paget (1768–1854) uttered the deathless line at Waterloo: "I have lost my leg, by God!" The Duke of Wellington replied: "By God, and have you!" Paget's son, Lord George Augustus Frederick Paget (1818–1880), survived intact the Charge of the Light Brigade at Balaklava and is not to be confused with Sir George Paget (1814–1899), Regius Professor of Medicine at Cambridge, who fathered two bishops besides Stephen (1855–1926), the vivisectionist author of *Experiments on Animals*. There is a monument to the first Marquis's leg at Plas Newydd which is visited by Welshmen living uneventful lives. Oxymoronically, the Isle of Man's coat-of-arms depicts three legs, alluding to a three-legged Manxman who would have had an advantage at Waterloo. The great Marquis died in the year of Lord Raglan's victory at Inkerman; after a surgical amputation at Waterloo, this same Raglan ordered: "Here, bring that arm back, there is a ring my wife gave me on the finger."

The year of the Battle of Balaklava has the same arithmetic sum as the year of the birth of Sarah Bernhardt who lost a leg. More astonishing is the coincidence of the ballerina Tanaquil LeClerq who lost the use of both legs after contracting polio in

1956: in 1944, aged fifteen, she had been chosen by her future husband Georges Balanchine to star at the Waldorf-Astoria Hotel in a ballet for the benefit of the March of Dimes, about a ballet student stricken with polio.

Christian Archibald Herter (1895–1966) walked with crutches after losing much of the use of his legs; he resigned as Secretary of State in 1961 on the fiftieth anniversary of the publication of *Biological Aspects of Human Problems* by his father, the physician Christian, Sr. (1865–1910). The elder Herter died on the centenary of the first Marquis of Anglesey's resignation from Parliament, four years before the leg incident at Waterloo.

In Havana in 1731 the Spanish captain Fandino cut off the ear of Robert Jenkins. Thenceforth that English seaman displayed his ear in an ornamental box, exciting admiration, sympathy, and indignation culminating in the War of Jenkins's Ear in 1739. In battle in 695 (having the same arithmetic sum as 1739) the general Leontius cut off the nose of his emperor who has gone down in history as Justinian II Rhinotmetus ("The Noseless"). Rhinotmetusness did not diminish his ability to fight, as the loss of a limb would have; and it did not affect his ability to govern, as the loss of a head often has. But it was an aggravation added upon constant harassment by the Bulgarians and Armenian Arabs. Justinian wanted Pope St. Sergius to endorse the second Trullan Council and abolish clerical celibacy. Sergius refused and soon enough the commander of the imperial bodyguard, Zacharias, on a trip to Rome had to avoid his own rebellious troops by hiding under the pope's bed. The nosed pope's moral victory over the noseless emperor was commemorated by a bust of Sergius at the Church of Santa Susanna which was rubbed so much for good luck that the nose came off.

In the 1554 conspiracy of the Kentish fanatic Sir Thomas Wyatt against Queen Mary, one of his lieutenants shot an arrow into the courtyard at Whitehall striking off part of the nose of an attorney of Lincoln's Inn. At the sight of the bleeding appendage, royal guardsmen cried out, "All is lost! Away! Away!" Courageous "Bloody" Mary Tudor cried back, "Fall to prayer!" and the day was won. The parboiled body of Wyatt was quartered and displayed in four parts of London. Mary had been betrothed to the Dauphin of the longest-nosed monarch on record, Francis I, at the age of two in 1518 when De Gomez first sighted the proboscis monkey of Borneo—which is addendum to Pascal's belief that the whole face of the earth would have been changed if Cleopatra's nose had been shorter. The centenary of Mary's marriage to Philip II of Spain saw the first performance of the tragedy *La Mort d'Agrippine* by Cyrano de Bergerac. A later Mary, the only daughter of George V, married Viscount Lascelles, who was left £3 million by Lord Clanricarde, a man able to flick out his tongue like a lizard and lick his nose. His ancestor, the first marquis and fifth earl of Clanricarde was named Ulick (1604–1657).

Any loss of physical parts tests one's mettle. Legends of headless saints exaggerate the point. But it is a point. When in 1763 D'Alembert mocked the story of St. Denis carrying his detached head two whole leagues, the Marquise Du Deffand remarked: "The distance does not matter; it is only the first step that counts." Moral detachment is more to be desired than physical detachment is to be feared. That at least is our gloss on the Savior's point about plucking out the eye and cutting off the hand. Language so graphic inevitably is most offensive and tasteless to those who are most carnal and vulgar.

A TERRIBLE SWIFT SWORD

As a youth, Winston Churchill told Violet Bonham-Carter: "We are all worms. But I do believe I am a glow-worm." He was the man for the world's worst cataclysm, as Lincoln was the man for our nation's defining moment. Both were, as the ancients were wont to say, "Tam Marte quam Minerva" or, paraphrased, as valiant as wise. Outside very providence more than coincidence, it is hard to explain such figures, and the mystery surely could not have been lost on the great men themselves. Their saving grace was to take their moment more seriously than they took themselves, and to take their own greatness in stride. When a boy asked him if he was really the greatest man in the world, Churchill grumbled, "Yes. Now buzz off." When Lincoln was accused of duplicity, he replied, "If I were two-faced, would I be wearing this one?" And in so saying, he embodied the existential golden mean between tragedy and comedy which saves a time of testing from unwinding into misery or absurdity.

Real wars like their real heroes are larger than myth, and

the circumstances attached to them surpass the stuff of legend. It was so even with the prolegomenon of the Civil War. Long before the capture of Fort Sumter, coincidence seemed to be setting the stage for our national drama. The leader of England's abolitionist movement, William Wilberforce, entered Parliament in 1780 at the same age Lincoln was when he settled in Illinois in 1830. Wilberforce died as Lincoln was appointed postmaster. At the time, Wilberforce was the world's foremost anti-slavery statesman. So, twenty-three years after slavery was eliminated in the British Empire, Wilberforce College was founded in western Ohio for the higher education of blacks. Oblivious to the coincidence, on that day in

Osawatomie, Kansas, three hundred pro-slavery men attacked forty of John Brown's followers.

In the Mexican War ten years before, an amazing array of military talent formed behind their generals Zachary Taylor and Winfield Scott, with names that would grow in prominence: Colonel Jefferson Davis, Lieutenant Ulysses S. Grant, and two with the rank of captain, George McClellan and Robert E. Lee. During his brilliant maneuvers at Cerro Gordo *en route* from Veracruz to Mexico City, Lee had Grant and McClellan under his command. Rather charmingly, the widow of Jefferson Davis, author of a belabored life of her husband in two volumes which was published in 1890, was a friend of the widow of George Armstrong Custer and they vacationed together in the Gramatan Hotel in Bronxville, New York. Another guest of the hotel was Theodore Roosevelt whose Southern mother had taught him to revere Jefferson Davis and who was awarded the Nobel Peace Prize in the year of Varina Davis's death.

McClellan notoriously hesitated at Antietam on September 17, 1862 in spite of the discovery of Confederate plans written on a paper which had been used to wrap some cigars. McClellan's cousin, Henry Brainerd McClellan, was chief of staff to the Confederate Major-General J. E. B. Stuart. This may not rank as much of a coincidence, since so many families were divided in their loyalties. Coincidence glares here however: Lee was born when Wilberforce's anti-slavery measure first carried in the House of Commons, Stuart was born when Wilberforce died, and Grant and McClellan died in 1885. On the same Fourth of July in 1863, the city of Vicksburg with 30,000 troops surrendered to Grant and the troops of Lee were defeated at Gettysburg.

Wilmer McLean certainly had reason to rue the strange workings of coincidence. He was a landowner in Virginia who watched with fascination and trepidation as the first Battle of Bull Run unfolded near his homestead in the summer of 1861. A year later, the second battle devastated his properties. Fed up, he chose to move to a quieter place unknown to the chariots of Mars. He removed family and possessions to the sleepy town of Appomattox. Things did not stay uneventful there. When the dust of battle settled, Lee surrendered to Grant in the parlor of Mr. McLean's house. Such inter-twinings and correlations gave a predictable ghostliness to the horror and heroism of those days.

On the fiftieth anniversary of Pasteur's successful treatment of a child for hydrophobia, a woman telephoned the editor of *The Richmond News Leader* to say that General Lee's bronze horse, on his monument in Richmond, was foaming at the mouth. A reporter investigated and found that a swarm of bees had built a hive around the bridle and summer heat had caused the honey to foam. Why the bees had chosen Lee's Traveller rather than Stonewall Jackson's Little Sorrel nearby, or any of the other horses on Monument Boulevard is, as they say, unclear. To military historians it may have seemed just a coincidence, but a fitting one. And so thought the Southern lady with a long memory who reported it as though she were Elisha witnessing the ascent of Elijah. No one in Richmond thought her foolish.

GREAT MINDS THINKING ALIKE

MANY HAVE READ THE EXPLANATORY NOTE OF 29 JUNE 1998 on Pope John Paul II's *motu proprio, Ad Tuendam Fidem,* issued by the Congregation for the Doctrine of the Faith, as chance would have it, on the centenary of suffrage in Norway and the election of the former king Milan as commander-in-chief of the Serbian army. One hundred years later the Norwegian government is almost totally female and the Serbian army is again a storm center of controversy. But these were not the subject of the doctrinal commentary. It sought rather to explain how truths are identified for all times and circumstances. So a footnote says, ". . . such an infallible teaching is thus objectively set forth by the whole episcopal body, understood in a diachronic and not necessarily merely synchronic sense."

In other words, formulations of a truth have to be understood in the context of a wide historical panorama as an *organum* applicable to all times and conditions, and not according to the predilections and perceptions of the moment. Synchrony is a coincidence of time; diachrony is inclusive of all

times. It does not help much to check out the dictionary and find as a gloss this remark of George P. Faust: "Historical (diachronic) linguistics is an honorable field of study; so is structural (synchronic) linguistics." More helpful are juicy *mots* of the venerable Simeon Potter: "A man may surely make a rational and satisfying synchronic or descriptive study of a language now or for any time in the past, but, if that study is to remain one hundred per cent synchronic, he must at no point ask or state the reason why, for that will ineluctably bring in diachronic or historical factors."

By extension, we could say that the Light Brigade at Balaklava might have been saved had they been more diachronic, but it is "not for us to reason why." And when Marshall Bosquet saw them and said "It is magnificent, but it is not war," he meant that it was great synchrony but not at all diachrony, language that might have been lost on the brave bleeding soldiers. Is it not both synchronic and diachronic that Lord Raglan, for whom the triple-seamed raglan sleeve is named, accused Lord Lucan after Balaklava the way Nero condemned his own Lucan (Marcus Annaeus Lucanus)?

All this is by way of introducing astonishing specimens of synchrony in the physical sciences. Jean Nicholas Sebastien Allamand, explicator of the phenomenon of the Leyden jar, died just as Russia and Austria were declaring war on Turkey. In 1769 as Eleazar Wheelock was founding Dartmouth College, James Watt invented the steam engine, Richard Arkwright invented the spinning frame, and Joseph Wedgewood opened his "Etruria" pottery works. The English chemist William Prout discovered hydrochloric acid in the stomach in the year of the proclamation of the Monroe Doctrine, a high point in the "Era of Good Feeling." Robert Wilhelm Bunsen, inventor of the Bunsen burner, was born in the year the Mississippi River flowed backwards after an earthquake in New Madrid, Missouri. Henry Sweet, founder of modem phonetics, died in 1912 when George Bernard Shaw presented *Pygmalion* featuring the professor of phonetics, Henry Higgins. In 1859, a twelve-year-old newspaper boy named Thomas Alva Edison working on the Grand Trunk Railway in Michigan, was rewarded for saving a stationmaster's son by being given a scholarship to an academy in Mount Clemens which serendipitously happened to specialize in the new science of telegraphy. On September 3, 1930, as Edison's electric passenger train was making its first trip on the Lackawanna tracks in New Jersey, Dieudonne Coste and Maurice Bellonte landed at Valley Stream, Long Island in the first direct flight from Paris to the United States.

Now synchrony yields to diachrony. I have noted elsewhere how in 1846 John Couch Adams and Urbain Jean Joseph Leverrier simultaneously calculated the position of the planet Neptune. In England, William Henry Fox Talbot announced a photographic process ("photogenic drawing") in 1839 exactly when Louis Jacques Daguerre announced to the Academy of Sciences his invention of the daguerreotype. Talbot also figured out the Persian cuneiform vowel system simultaneously with the Irish Orientalist Edward Hincks and the English Assyriologist Henry Creswicke Rawlinson, all of whom acted without any collusion. In 1860 Antonio Pacinotti in Italy and Zenobe Theophile Gramme in Belgium simultaneously invented the ring winding which Gramme would use on his dynamo ten years later.

Correlations like these are hyper-synchronic. Only an amalgam of arrogance and presumption would claim to know how and why these moments meshed as they did. A plausible suggestion is that these men absorbed the intentions of nature's timeless laws and transcended the limits of insular perspective so that their insights were the material glimmerings of the universal lamp of knowledge. When great minds are alike, it is synchrony strutting like a peacock. When great minds think alike, it is diachrony like a peacock in full display.

DOWN TO THE
SEA IN SHIPS

THE COVERDALE TRANSLATION OF PSALM 107:23
sonorously extols them "that go down to the sea in ships, and
occupy their business in great waters." The lines have been in-
toned over countless bodies being committed to an ocean
grave. An aggrieved Prince of Wales read those words at the funeral of Lord Mountbatten of Burma whose grandfather, Prince
Alexander of Battenberg, died on the 300th anniversary of the
Spanish Armada and whose elder brother, the second Marquis
of Milford Haven, died on the 350th anniversary of the same.

Nothing in literature is older than the saga of the sea. Start
with Genesis. Even those who deny that the Spirit of the Lord
moved upon the face of the waters, assume that all life started
as acquatic amoebae and shrimps that gradually got legs. I can
think of no more brilliant example of genius on the subject
than Ronald Knox's essay on "The Greeks at Sea", the whole
point of which is that the ancient Greeks really did not like
sailing. They wrote gorgeously stolid Dorian odes to the waves,
and hymned of the Hellespont and Aegospotami as we still do

today with reduced diction in travel brochures; but the Greeks wrote with foreboding. The Jews were even more suspicious of the great waters and thought that the Red Sea's best moment was when it split. Otherwise, it was merely a playground for the rambunctious Phoenicians.

Odd and tragic coincidences in maritime history render a little more plausible the breathless meters of James Elroy Flecker (1884–1915): "The dragon-green, the luminous, the dark, the serpent-haunted sea." That sea haunts us, too, especially with the realization that Flecker died in the year of the loss of 1,154 lives on the *Lusitania*. More odd than tragic is this: the United States Secretary of State William Jennings Bryan (in H. L. Mencken's estimation "The National Tear-Duct") officially protested the ship's sinking on May 13, 1915 which was the 400th anniversary, to the day, of the marriage of the Duke of Suffolk to Mary, the widow of Louis XII and sister of Henry VIII, after she had spurned the hand of the Archduke Charles. There is something ominous even in the name of the great hydrologist of the Massachusetts Institute of Technology who set the standards for water purification: Thomas Drown (1842–1904). Swinburne capitalized on the pathos: ". . . the place of the slaying of Itylus / The feast of Daulis, the Thracian sea." And a singularly melancholy fact about the sea is that Swinburne did not end up in it.

With the sea, as with its undulating waves themselves, there seems to be no up without a down. On August 10, 1790 Captain Robert Gray completed the first circumnavigation of the world by an American vessel, sailing into Boston Harbor on the *Columbia* laden with coveted tea and greeted with euphoria by the local tea drinkers. But after July 20, 1793 when he returned to

the same harbor from his second circumnavigation of this shining planet, those of a certain political stripe in the welcoming crowd were soon silenced by news of Thomas Jefferson's resignation as Secretary of State on the same day. In a similar vein, the happy progress of the Panama Canal was mitigated by the yellow fever. The building of the Suez Canal for the improvement of portage was no less benighted. Ferdinand Marie de Lesseps (1805–1894), pioneer of its construction, had been sent as the French minister plenipotentiary to negotiate with Giuseppe Mazzini (1805–1872) during the Italian Risorgimento. They were born in the same year, and in the year of the negotiations a son named Charles was born to de Lesseps. When Charles attained his majority, he and his father were found guilty of misusing investment monies, which took much of the thrill out of the sight of ships sailing through the new canal. Of course Ferdinand's putterings in Panama were a total bust.

The first and last voyage of the *Titanic* in 1912 did not increase confidence in seafaring; but most of the world has forgotten, if it ever remembered, the loss of a thousand lives in the sinking of a Japanese steamer in the same year. Over-exercised numerologists may darkly warn that the numerical sum of 1912 is 13, but all was not grim, or unlucky if you will, in that year. On his fortieth birthday, the first of September in 1912, while sailing out of Belfast on the *King Frederick VII* which was named for the last of the Oldenburg line, Captain Daniel Saunders recovered from the sea incarnadine a bottle containing a message. His crewmen gathered about and all fell silent at what they read: it was the notice of Captain Saunder's birth written those forty years before in the hand of his own proud father.

Stunning as that coincidence was in the records of such things, a further gloss is put on it by realization that it happened in the year of the death of the successor of childless Frederick VII, Frederick VIII, the son of the fourth son of the Duke of Schleswig-Holstein-Sonderburg-Glucksburg, Christian IX, who had married the daughter of the Prince of Hesse-Cassel in the year of the birth of the abovementioned hydrologist Thomas Drown and whose own father, Christian VIII, had been such a close friend of Kierkegaard and putatively the father of Hans Christian Andersen.

So the sea is not consistently as cruel as the darker bits of Greek narrative poetry would have it. There have been times, pace *A Midsummer Night's Dream*, when "the rude sea grew civil." But that was only in fancy, when a mermaid sang on a dolphin's back. Far stranger and more glorious revelations have come with the turning of tides and wailing of winds. It is all part of the Good News for which Genesis was the prelude. They that occupy their business in great waters should not be anxious but should rejoice that real raging waves in ancient Galilee grew civil at a rebuke from their very God.

A MORE
DELIGHTFUL VISION

WOULD ANYONE LIKE A SURE-FIRE FORMULA FOR A
Broadway hit? I think this fits the bill: a one-act play in which
Edmund Burke and Marie Antoinette are shipwrecked on a
desert island. The scene is improbable, but the theatre would
not be theatrical were it the pantheon of probability and the
loggia of logic. Burke himself set the tone for such a drama in
one of his passages so memorable that it is quoted the world
over by instinct at the first mention of his name. That venerable Nestor (I see his eyes welling up) writes in *Reflections on the
Revolution in France*:

> It is now sixteen or seventeen years since I saw the Queen of
> France, then the Dauphiness, at Versailles; and surely never
> lighted this orb, which she hardly seemed to touch, a more
> delightful vision. I saw her just above the horizon, decorating
> and cheering the elevated sphere she just began to move in,—
> glittering like the morning star, full of life, and splendour, and
> joy . . . Little did I dream that I should have lived to see
> disasters fallen upon her in a nation of gallant men, in a nation

of men of honour, and of cavaliers. I thought ten thousand swords must have leaped from their scabbards to avenge even a look that threatened her with insult. But the age of chivalry is gone. That of sophisters, economists, and calculators, has succeeded; and the glory of Europe is extinguished for ever.

My Broadway drama would begin with a simulation of the immediate aftermath of the Lisbon earthquake, November 2, 1755. For, on that day of indelible catastrophe whose physical fires lit the way for the cynical *philosophes*, as if Mother Nature had gone into an agonizing labor of unmeasured tremors and incalculable issue, a child was born in Austria and the child's name was Marie Antoinette Josephe Jeanne. Hilaire Belloc begins her biography with mention of the earthquake: "Sudden causes of change are always accompanied by coincidence. Allied forces invariably converge upon the main cause of change and unite for a common effort."

As the future Queen of France lay in her cradle, the University of Moscow was chartered and a youth named Charles Cornwallis was commissioned in the British army. Readers already will have figured out why I mention Cornwallis. His surrender at Yorktown, for which he would soon atone with a series of brilliant victories in India over Tippoo Sahib, wrought three days later the official end of the American Revolutionary War and on that same day of October 22 in 1781, Marie Antoinette gave birth to the first Dauphin, Louis Joseph Xavier; her brother Emperor Joseph II issued the Edict of Toleration in Austria; and Count Jean Frédéric Phélippeaux, Compte de Maurepas, who had been Louis XIV's first prime minister, died. It was a congested day on the highway of history. The French

negotiator at Yorktown was Count Hans Axel von Fersen, actually the son of the Swedish field marshall Count Fredrik Axel
von Fersen, born the same year as Marie Antoinette and linked
romantically to her by many rumors. When Louis XVI and his
queen attempted to flee France, only to be caught at Varennes,
the coachman was this same Count von Fersen in disguise. His
fate was little more fortunate than the calumniated Queen's,
being killed in a populist revolt of 1810 in grim consequence of
his unpopularity.

On the centenary of the events at Yorktown, which also saw
the felicitous rise of the Bodawpaya dynasty in Burma, Tunisia
became a French protectorate. In the golden age of the Bodaw-
payas, Rudyard Kipling would pen his immortal couplet: "By
the old Moulmein Pagoda, lookin' eastward to the sea, / There's
a Burma girl a-settin', and I know she thinks o' me . . ." Mixed
are my emotions when I think of Tunisia for it was there, near
the site where Aeneas met Queen Dido that I once nearly died
from food poisoning. The melancholy lament of Aeneas to the
Queen of Carthage, like Kipling's nostalgia for the Burma girl,

could easily be translated to the lips of Burke addressing the ghost of Marie Antoinette, and I must say that the Virgilian tear-jerker kept coming to me in my feverish hours in Tunis: "Infandum, regina, iubes renovare dolorem." "You bid, O Queen, the retelling of a grief too deep for words." Infandum. Probably the finest example of the participle of necessity in all Latin grammar, and sufficient alone to qualify Virgil as the Roman Kipling, as Burke might be the British Virgil.

The temporary mausoleum of Louis and Marie in Paris, erected by Charles X, is just across the street from the Church of St. Augustin, where the Abbé Huvelin reconciled Charles de Foucauld to the Church, launching him on his heroic career with a pilgrimage to the Holy Land on the centenary of the fall of the Bastille. The Tuaregs tribesmen who killed him in North Africa during the Holy War of the Senoussi were as cruel and senseless as the hags knitting at the guillotine of Marie Antoinette.

There are those who have knelt at her tenantless tomb upon reading the engraved words from her last will and testament, sentiments whose piety correct any shortsightedness in her pubescent social vision. Buried in the geranium garden outside are the Swiss Guards who were butchered defending the king and queen at the Tuileries on August 10, 1792. Chivalry was not dead so long as they lived, though dead upon dead it was in the hearts of those who so obscenely taunted in captivity the queen and, worse, the Princess de Lamballe. On the seventy-fifth anniversary of the Swiss Guard massacre, John Surratt was detained in a federal prison accused of conspiring in the assassination of Lincoln, although the jury had voted for acquittal. Burke's fearsome hegemony of sophisters, economists and calculators, have made our own government a baby-boomer coven of moral deconstruction. But the glory may not be gone for ever. Not if children are taught to read once more the likes of Burke. At least on this the great Burke may not have had the last word.

OLD BONEY

A reflection of Mark Twain abides: "How often we recall with regret that Napoleon once shot at a magazine editor and missed him and killed a publisher. But we remember with charity that his intentions were good." Sympathetic words, these, spurring the hope that my list of items about Napoleon Bonaparte, the Boney of so many Anglo-Saxon nightmares, will not suffer on the Procrustean bed of the editor's desk.

Of all his books, Twain loved best his biography of Joan of Arc, and so it is meet and right to reflect that Napoleon revived the dormant cult of Joan, putting up a statue to her in Orleans in 1803. Coincidentally, one hundred years later, not a year less or more, Marshall Foch stunned France by suggesting that Napoleon had lacked measure. Napoleon's genius is certain. His vulgarity was evident long before he reminisced about Josephine's physiognomy the way he did in his last exile. That he was more the natural child of fate than the adopted child of circumstance has volumes of attestation. If all the strange events of his life were nothing but coincidental, their sheer number would itself be a paramount coincidence.

In the enthusiasm of so many for their Emperor, moderation was not a virtue. Their representative figure, the legendary soldier Nicholas Chauvin, for whom chauvinism is named, was delighted to have been wounded seventeen times for Napoleon. After the Russian disaster, the notorious Twenty-ninth Bulletin from the front neglected to mention the half-million French casualties and announced, "His Majesty's health has never been better." Messianism attached itself to Napoleon's alarums and excursions with facts like these: he became First Counsel on a Friday in 1797, crowned himself Emperor on a Friday in 1804, and began his journey to St. Helena on a Friday in 1815. As a capstone to all that, the British Crown ceded possession of his grave to the King of France on a Friday in 1821. On July 15, 1915, one hundred years to the day after Napoleon's surrender, Austro-German forces like jagged lightning launched their offensive along the Eastern Front.

The vessel on which the British received Napoleon's surrender was the "H. M. S. Bellerophon." This was not by design, at least not by human design. I point this out because Bellerophon in Greek mythology was the heroic slayer of the Chimera. Napoleon's dejection is captured poignantly in the splendid painting "Napoleon on Board the Bellerophon." The artist,

John James Chalon (1778–1854) coincidently bore the name of the princely house of Burgundy whose last Orange prince, Philibert de Chalon turned so violently against Francis I and attained much distinction at Fuenterrabia in 1523. That morose day of Napoleon's surrender also witnessed one of history's grandest homophonic sentences, a homophone being, we might say, a verbal coincidence. It happened thusly. Napoleon stood silent on the deck for a painful while and then muttered with resignation: "Cast off, it is time to go." Only the Corsican said it in his accented French which he had learned at the age of ten: "A l'eau, c'est l'heure." A young British sailor standing on deck knew not the gilded tongue of mankind's golden race. Under the impression that the fallen emperor was speaking English, the sailor was flattered by what he mistook for familiarity and later reported that Napoleon had the courtesy to address him, "Hello, sailor." On the 150th anniversary of that day, the spacecraft Mariner 4 sent back its first photographs of the planet named for the Roman god of war.

Five years before his famous homophone, and just after the United States repealed its Non-Intercourse Act of 1809, Napoleon took in marriage the Archduchess Marie Louise of Austria. With the world's attention riveted on that spectacle, a light-boned waist corset was invented and displayed in Paris with little fanfare, but it would have an immeasurable impact on the world of fashion. Josephine may have been left by the wayside, but her daughter Hortense Beauharnais gave birth to the future Napoleon III. As he was dying from cancer of the stomach, he regularly reviewed his troops on horseback, propped up by one of the light-boned waist corsets invented in 1810. Chalon was not around to paint that wistful scene, as he died in the year the third Napoleon committed France to the Crimean War.

When he was isolated on St. Helena, Napoleon was a little like Chateaubriand of whom Talleyrand said, "He thinks himself deaf because he no longer hears himself talked of." Thinking back about his drenched battlefields and vacant thrones, that *anax andron* would have agreed with the modern babyboomer wisdom: "Power tends to corrupt. Absolute power is kind of neat." But he was not heartless. Far from it. His last testament pulled on Gallican heartstrings by willing that his own and very heart be buried by the Seine among the people he had loved so well. If it was the last breath of his olympian cynicism, it was sincere cynicism, a Half-Messiah's way of saying, "My word is half-truth." The half-truths of the immoral are not worse than the whole lies of the amoral who govern much of politics now. The latter do not want to be Messiahs. They only want power to shoot the publishers. Editors in their crosshairs are not worth a bullet.

WHEN THE
CURTAIN FALLS

SAGES HAVE OBSERVED THAT WHILE THE PUBLIC SCENE
is afflicted with countless personalities who are false tinsel, only
in Hollywood are people genuine tinsel. Falseness is not a universal trait of actors; although Samuel Goldwyn did say that in
Hollywood an oral contract is not worth the paper it is written
on. For various reasons, and irreasons, actors everywhere have
been scorned as much as they have been adulated. Alfred Hitchcock told a reporter: "I deny that I ever said that actors are cattle.
What I said was, 'Actors should be treated like cattle.'"

The stage has been the scene of coincidences too dramatic
for any playwright trying for realism. Think of Molière dying on
stage in 1673 at the *Academie Francaise* in the title role of his
own "La Malade Imaginaire." That was an instance of the actor
being too sincere for the part. And while thousands took to the
road in reaction to the verisimilitude of Orson Welles's radio
broadcast of an adaptation of the H.G. Wells story *War of the
Worlds*, no one noticed a chilling coincidence with a legitimate
panic: Welles broadcast his drama on October 30, 1938 and on

October 30, 1838 the murder of seventy Mormons in Missouri caused a flight of 15,000 of their co-religionists toward Illinois. Hardly less enigmatic was the death in 1944 of Sir John Martin Harvey, the actor and producer perhaps most memorable for his staging of *Scaramouche*: he expired on the very eve of the four hundredth birthday of that other Harvey, Gabriel, father of the English hexameter. Sir John was active in Sir Henry Irving's company when yet another Harvey, Edmund, was born in America in 1887; the physiologist studied the esoteric phenomenon of light production of animals, which curiosity becomes all the more intense in consequence of the eponymous giant rabbit in the popular play *Harvey*.

The Italian actress Eleonora Duse, born in 1859, returned to the stage after a twelve-year hiatus which began in 1909, and died in Pittsburgh while on tour in 1924 on the same day that the novelist Mary Mackay ("Marie Corelli") who had been born four years before Duse, died in Stratford-on-Avon. Mackay's pseudonymous surname was that of the violinist Arcangelo, to whom the invention of the concerto grosso is credited. Errol Flynn was born in the first year of Duse's temporary retreat from the stage and died on the centenary of her birth and the bicentenary of the imprisonment of Captain William Bligh of the "Bounty" who, in his turn, was born one year after the centenary of Arcangelo Corelli. The heart-throb Flynn who played Fletcher Christian in "Mutiny on the Bounty" was descended on his mother's side from Midshipman Young, a mutineer on the actual ship. Having starred as Bligh in the motion picture, Charles Laughton died on the seventy-fifth anniversary of the birth of Edmund Harvey who had died three years earlier on the centenary of the birth of Duse.

Captain William Bligh was the object of Mr. Christian's mutinous regard precisely ten years before the birth of Aleksandr Sergeevich Pushkin, whose *Boris Godunov* provided the book for Musorgski's opera. Pushkin's great-grandmother had a child by the Ethiopian ambassador to St. Petersburg. In an uncanny parallelism, the modern author and actor Peter Usti-nov, of a Russian family, had an Ethiopian grandmother. A decade apart like the mutiny on the Bounty and the birth of Pushkin, are the birthdays of the great English actress Margaret Rutherford, in 1892, and the Russian novelist Mikhail Alexandrovich Sholokhov, in 1902. Although Dame Margaret is remembered for her understated drollness, she was afflicted with painful depressions which were complicated when her adopted son, who was black, had a sex-change operation and became a Methodist.

Laurence Olivier, born five years after Sholokhov, made his debut when he was nine in an amateur performance of *Julius Caesar* attended by Ellen Terry. The legendary figure of the London stage had made her own debut, also at the age of nine, in the presence of Queen Victoria. On Victoria's wedding day, February 10 in 1840, the Duke of Cambridge, Prince George, met Sarah Louisa Fairbrother, the daughter of a London printer. The winsome lady had become an actress in the Drury Lane

Theatre ten years earlier, being the same span of time separating the Bounty mutiny and the birth of Pushkin. The prince and the printerette would marry not without controversy. Parenthetically, the wedding of the Duke of Kent and Katherine Worsley in 1961 was also the occasion of the second meeting of the Count of Barcelona and Princess Sofia of Greece who now reign as King and Queen of Spain.

In the year of Grover Cleveland's re-election, 1892, when Margaret Rutherford made her debut in the world, Prince Albert of Monaco, having received an annulment of his marriage to Lady Mary Douglas Hamilton, married the widow of the Duc de Richelieu, the former Alice Heine, making her the first American wife of a reigning European prince. Alice was an amateur actress and patron of the arts. In the year of the re-election of Dwight Eisenhower, 1956, Prince Rainier of Monaco married the American actress Grace Kelly.

Several years ago I met a college student who had never heard of Edith Piaf. Lacunae like that account to no little degree for much of the collapse of the grand tradition of the stage. In one of those coincidences whose theatricality stretch the credibility of the theatre to the point of melodrama, Piaf and Jean Cocteau died of natural causes on the same *triste* eleventh of October in 1963. She was 47 and he was 74. Not to be too gaudy about the coincidence, Cocteau was born on the centenary of the mutiny on the H.M.S. Bounty.

MORE VARIETIES OF RELIGIOUS EXPERIENCE

FELICITOUS ARRANGEMENTS ALLOWED ME AS A STUDENT to repair weekly to practice the piano in a house by the Folly Bridge on the site in Oxford where Roger Bacon had conducted scientific experiments in the thirteenth century. Bacon was a polymath if ever there was one between Aristotle and Leonardo da Vinci. His philosophy and theology (having introduced the schema of Aristotle to the University of Paris) had tough competition from the pyrotechnics of what he provocatively called *domina omnium scientiarum*—the experimental science which through him gave Europe gunpowder, thermometers, and a proto-telescope.

A fine line separates *domina* and *regina* (theology being *regina omnium scientiarum*) but it makes all the difference between truths and the Source of all truth. In 1941 in *Science, Philosophy and Religion*, Einstein said, "Science without religion is lame; religion without science is blind." Francis Bacon would not at all have been surprised that through the myriad corridors of religion would pass a bewildering array of coincidental happenstances.

Bacon's own nephew, the English Carmelite author of more than one hundred and twenty commentaries, was named Baconthorpe. He died in 1346; that is fifty-two years after his uncle's death. Thomas Beckett died in 1170 at the age of fifty-two. And by a larger symmetry Beckett shared a baptismal name with Thomas More: both contended against monarchs named Henry, both had been close friends of their king, and both were canonized martyrs for their protestation of the Church's rights against royal usurpation. The 308 years between the death of Beckett and the birth of More matches the number of priests in the Roman Catholic diocese of Hexham and Newcastle as of 1992. The sum of those years, 2,648, is equivalent to the year B.C. of the completion of the pyramid of Zoser at Saggara.

In the pageant of religion, one's arbitrary selection of coincidences will often be considered a result of some prejudice inseparable from a governing theological perspective. The dismal Dean Inge was of that opinion, because he was also minded that popular religions were philosophies enslaved by superstition. That notwithstanding, one has to admit a very odd coincidence of opposites which issues from the seventeenth century. In 1651, Thomas Goodwin, a Congregationalist chaplain to the Lord Protector who ministered at his death bed, wrote a book entitled *The Heart of Christ in Heaven toward sinners on earth: or, A Treatise demonstrating the gracious disposition and tender affection of Christ in His human Nature, now in glory, unto His members, under all sorts of infirmities, either of sin or misery.* Although it was meant to serve the severely polemical purposes of Oliver Cromwell, on numerous points and in many phrases it was uncannily similar to Catholic writings of St. Margaret Mary Alacoque and St. Claude

de la Colombiere on the mystical theology of the Sacred Heart. In unlikeliness, this parallels the almost identical appearance of Houdon's statue of Francois Marie Arouet and Cabuchet's statue of Jean Marie Vianney. Arouet, having assumed the name Voltaire, became the paramount patron of skeptics in the "Age of Reason" while Vianney, the Cure d'Ars, is the Church's canonized patron of parish priests. Inasmuch as Vianney was born on the centenary of Newton's completion of the *Principia* and died on the centenary of the publication of Voltaire's *Candide*, it is fetching that the story of the apple falling on Newton's head was spread by Voltaire after he heard it from the great man's stepniece and that he was present at the burial of Newton in Westminster Abbey. The Russian chiliast, Baroness Barbara von Krudener, who was so very unlike Voltaire in her embrace of Swedenborgianism, was born in the year he published the *Dictionnaire Philosophique*.

By its essential expansiveness, Catholicity is the most fertile ground for the congruence of superficial incongruities. The sum of the numbers of the year Goodwin's book was published is the same as the sum of 1750 in which year John Connolly was born. This first resident Bishop of New York, an Irishman, had been English language secretary in Italy to the Cardinal Prince Henry of York; the Cardinal's brother was "Bonnie Prince Charlie" and his father was the "Old Pretender", James III of Scotland. Their tomb by Canova, in St. Peter's Basilica in Rome, was repaired in recent years with a gift of Queen Elizabeth the Queen Mother, who was born the daughter of the 14th Earl of Strathmore and Kinghorne on the 150th anniversary of the birth of Bishop Connolly.

Numerologists have long pondered the significance of 153, which is the number of fish recorded in the New Testament account of John 21: 10–11, corresponding to the total known number of species of fish in the world according to the *Halieutica* of Oppian. Such speculation courts obscurantism which we have sworn on the Altar of the Muses to fight at all costs. There remains a number that permeates all layers of potent thoughts and events. Christ spoke seven times from the Cross; there were seven days of creation, seven miraculous signs in the Gospel according to St. John, seven virtues theological and cardinal, seven deadly sins, seven petitions in the Our Father, seven churches addressed in the Book of Revelation, seven sorrows of the Virgin Mary, and seven gifts of the Holy Spirit. These should inspire and not perplex, so long as we bear in mind that there are seven causes of anxiety according to St. Francis de Sales. It would not be to the point to list them here, but we can at least note that St. Francis, with his cousin Louis, embarked upon the recovery of the Chablais on the three hundredth anniversary of the death of Roger Bacon.

A BRIDGE
TO THE FUTURE

THE PROMISE TO "BUILD A BRIDGE TO THE FUTURE" became a mantra in 1990s politics. It is less cogent than Longfellow's maxim in *The Golden Legend* about not crossing a bridge until you come to it. The future needs no bridge. It comes slowly for the impatient and with daunting haste for the cautious who would cross any bridge to it like the poor prisoners being conducted over the Bridge of Sighs. One can greet the future. One cannot go out to it the way you can go from the Bronx to the New Jersey Palisades. Besides, if any truly sane and civilized politician could build a bridge to some other time he would build it to the second half of the thirteenth century, thus winning the support of admirers of Louis IX and perpendicular Gothic.

Commonly, a bridge is a structure built to cross a body of water. A unique exception to this rule was the former London Bridge rebuilt in 1831 by the great John Rennie, the work on which was actually completed by his sons John and George. His bridge did indeed span the Thames, but it was purchased by an

American land developer who removed it to an Arizona desert as a tourist attraction in 1973, the bridge being erected first and water placed under it later. The developer mistakenly supposed the London Bridge was the Tower Bridge, but it became a public relations success nonetheless, showing that the man made up in commercial shrewdness what he may have lacked in general culture.

The Pons Aemilius, the first masonry arch across the Tiber begun in 179 B.C., was no less a technical marvel than what was the longest reinforced concrete bridge when it was completed in 1911: the Risorgimento, which coincidentally spanned the same watery vein. Two years later in Missouri, the St. Louis Municipal Bridge was dedicated concurrently with the appointment of England's poet laureate, Robert Bridges. The numerical sum of the year of his birth, 1844, multiplied by 10, is identical to the length in feet of the Philadelphia-Camden Bridge over the Delaware River. The precursor of the St. Louis Municipal Bridge, which was of simple truss design, was a steel arch structure completed in 1871 and designed by James Buchanan Eads, who also planned the bridge over the Isthmus of Tehuantepec. He died in the Bahamas on March 6, 1887 as Henry Ward Beecher died in Brooklyn. And Brooklyn's phenomenal suspension bridge was completed simultaneously with the cantilevered railway bridge at Niagara Falls.

Ralph Waldo Emerson, having lyricized "the rude bridge that arched the flood", published *Representative Men* in 1850 as the tubular girder Britannia Bridge was dedicated over the Menai Strait in Wales, whose inhabitants in moral darkness had worshiped the water. The cost of the Ambassador Bridge across the Detroit River between the United States and

Canada was $20,000,000, identical to the estimated damages of the great New York City fire of 1835 and the price paid for the Philippine Islands. The Hell Gate Bridge over the East River in New York, the Interstate Bridge between Oregon and Washington, the Manhattan State Bridge in Chattanooga, the Ohio River Bridge at Metropolis in Illinois, the Quebec Bridge, and the Sciotoville (Ohio) Bridge, all were built in 1917. And the Outerbridge Crossing Bridge at Staten Island really is the outer bridge crossing although its name honors the Outerbridge family of New Jersey.

The Pecos Viaduct in Texas, built on Euclidean principles, is 323 feet high, and Euclid was born in 323 A.D. Quite apposite then is this curiosity: the fifth proposition of Euclid's first book is so difficult to "get over", for students not mathematically inclined, that it has been known since the Middle Ages as the "pons asinorum", or bridge of asses.

The longest suspension span of any bridge is that of the Humber Estuary Bridge in England, stretching 1410 metres which, if converted to years, is the year in which the Pisan cardinals declared that the pirate Baldassare Cossa was Pope John XXIII, Pontifex Maximus. That title of greatest bridge builder, renounced by the anti-pope in 1415, may have been a pun on an Osco-Umbrian term for a sacrificial offering. It had been used for the high priest since pagan Roman times. Satirized by Tertullian, it became a papal laurel around the fifth Christian century. The Battle of the Milvian Bridge changed papal history in 313, which number when converted to feet equals the span of the concrete arch Grafton Bridge in Auckland, New Zealand.

Macaulay was a Protestant and a Whig, but in 1840, the year England took formal possession of New Zealand, he wrote in his essay on von Ranke: "She (the Roman Catholic Church) may still exist in undiminished vigour when some traveler from New Zealand shall, in the midst of a vast solitude, take his stand on a broken arch of London bridge to sketch the ruins of St. Paul's." Macaulay was actually working from Sarah Taylor Austin's translation of von Ranke's *Die Römischen Päpste*. That brilliant wife of the jurist John Austin also translated Guizot's *Discours sur l'Histoire de la Révolution d'Angleterre* which was published ten years later at the time of the dedication of the Menai Straight bridge. Even prescient Macaulay did not predict that exactly one hundred years after penning his words, a 42-mph storm would send the four-month-old Tacoma Narrows Bridge crashing into Puget Sound, a result of aerodynamic flaws. Nor did Macaulay expect that before the end of the twentieth century the broken arch which he lyricized would be in Lake Havasu City, Arizona.

HEIRS TO THE HAIRLESS

DR. MARTIN ROUTH, PRESIDENT OF MAGDALEN COLLEGE for sixty-three years, was the last Oxford don to wear a wig in the eighteenth-century style, and this he did until he died in his hundredth year in 1854. He had been born on the twenty-fifth anniversary of the death of Peter the Great who banned beards from the imperial court, while encouraging court wigs. As St. Petersburg is the Liverpool of Russia, it is intriguing to learn from philology that the local Liverpudlian accent pronounces "hair and heir" and "hairpiece and herpes" the same.

Received opinion has it that hair loss is in proportion to intelligence. One thinks just off the top of one's head of: William Shakespeare, William Cullen Bryant, Herbert Spencer, Octave Crémazie, Wilbur Wright, and Dwight David Eisenhower. The bearded Bard of Avon seems to have been a bit defensive about his alopecia for he says in his *Comedy of Errors*: "There's many a man hath more hair than wit." It may well be that the incorporeal angels, at least in the highest and most splendid choirs, would appear to us as totally bald by virtue of their perfect intelligence. Hair, on the other hand, is a liability. Absalom, never to be equated in I.Q. with the angels, was doomed when his rampant follicles got caught up in the branches of an oak tree. Traditional iconography usually shows St. Paul as quite depilated and his precursor Elisha surely was, for he conjured up two she-bears to tear apart forty-two obnoxious children for the first bald joke mentioned in history. "Go up thou bald head" (2 Kings 2:23) is a fragile jest, but something may have been lost in translation. At Athens, St. Paul converted Dionysius the Areopagite, a man frequently confused with Dionysius the Pseudo-Areopagite, whose writing could have been lost to the world without the Latin translations of Erigena, who was funded in the ninth century by Charles the Bald.

Hair loss is not an infallible sign of sanctity, but it approaches godliness. By a catachretic exegesis of God's "hair like wool" in the Apocalypse, Rastafarian sectaries have concluded that God is negroid; but if we are respectful of metaphors, nothing in the Apocalypse will prove the presence of hair in heaven.

As anyone familiar with the Duke de Berry's *Book of Hours* can see, vain medieval women shaved the top front of their heads to increase their sex appeal. But hair is more generally associated with such appeal, at least among women. St. Paul tolerated it only when it was covered, and tonsure has long been the style of a life of perfection. After vain Julius Caesar's success over Pompey on the plains of Pharsalia, the Roman Senate voted him permission to wear the laurel wreath all the time, thus concealing his bald spot. Suetonius writes that he had been accustomed to combing the few strands of his hair forward, ". . . and of all the honours voted him by the Senate and

People, none pleased him so much as the privilege of wearing a laurel wreath on all occasions." After smallpox, Elizabeth I took to hairpieces and the Queen of Scots wore a wig to her execution in Fotheringay Castle. In his *History of the English-Speaking Peoples*, Churchill describes how her severed head dropped, leaving the executioner holding nothing but  the chignon. This romantic Mary was born coincidentally on the bicentenary of the death of Snorri Sturluson; his epic *Heimskringla* is virtually a hymn to the Norwegian kings who were congenitally hirsute from Harald the Fairhaired up to the year 1177 when bald intelligence entered the royal succession.

A man's wig, plaited with a queue and tied with a black ribbon, was the fashion of George Washington and other founding fathers. One fabled exception was Benjamin Franklin, whose bust of him shown wigless was venerated in the Cathedral of Notre Dame during the Reign of Terror. In 1761 Franklin happened to have been in London representing the Pennsylvania Assembly on tax matters concerning proprietary estates when Hogarth published his engravings of *Five Orders of Periwigs*. The wizard Franklin ordered numerous wigs in the French style. Fifteen years later as representative of his new nation and adulated as a man *bien dans sa peau*, he preferred a cap of marten fur and even appeared baldpated before Louis XVI, styling himself a

"Quaker." Nonetheless, his accounts while at the Hôtel d'Hambourg show expenditures for several wigs which he may have worn when not in a Rousseauan mood. Far different in attitude was the son of the poetess Lady Mary Wortley Montagu, Edward, a rather eccentric Arabic scholar and explorer who purchased in Paris a wig made completely of iron, which his mother admired for its verisimilitude. At the age of sixty-three, he died as Franklin was signing the Declaration of Independence. The plaited wig originally was peculiar to the army, probably because of its convenience, and was called the "Ramillie" after the 1706 Battle of Ramillies won by the first Duke of Marlborough on 23 May. Such was being worn by the duke's equerry when his entire head was sheered off by a cannonball as he was holding the duke's stirrup. The ninth duke was a cousin of the wigless Winston Churchill who not only described the wig of Mary, Queen of Scots, but also painted a picture of soldiers fighting at Blenheim wearing the Ramillie piece.

In nineteenth-century New York, Bishop Hughes and Cardinal McCloskey sported toupees without incident, unlike Archbishop Cosmo Gordon Lang of the Church of England, whose wig got caught in a chandelier in the episcopal palace at York in 1908. Exactly three hundred years after the birth of the gradually glabrous Elizabeth I, the prematurely bald future Cardinal Henry Manning wrote: "Nine-tenths of our bishops and priests neither know nor care more for a Bishop's wig than for a broccoli-head." Words these were that would come to haunt him, but true words nonetheless. It is important that they be so for, if bewigged Dr. Routh ever said anything memorable, it was his parting advice to a youth who had asked for some wisdom to support him on life's long journey: "Always verify your quotations."

TAKING FLIGHT

IN THE MOTION PICTURE, THE MONSTER "GODZILLA" IS shown stomping on my neighborhood and toppling the Chrysler Building onto my bedroom. The scenes look realistic through the use of computer technology. Special effects in the film *King Kong* of 1933, which ended on the nearby Empire State Building, were crude by comparison, but the script had memorable lines the finest of which was the last: "It wasn't the aeroplanes; beauty killed the beast." That notwithstanding, if Beauty was the formal cause, as moral philosophers might say, the airplanes were the material agents. *King Kong* ornamented the silver screen on the tenth birthday of Charles "Chuck" Yeager. I speak of the brigadier general and aviator who broke the sound barrier in his Bell X–1 "Glamorous Glennis" on October 14, 1947, being to the very day the 881st anniversary of the Battle of Hastings and the thirty-fifth anniversary of Joseph Schrank's attempt to assassinate Theodore Roosevelt, the first President to fly.

I suppose we could fabricate a mystique about all that by virtue of the coincidences at play. Orville Wright died twenty-five years after Yeager's birth. Five years later, Yeager set a new speed record in a rocket-powered plane at 1600 m.p.h. on December 16, the eve of the fiftieth anniversary of the Wright brothers' four famous flights at Kitty Hawk. Orville and Wilbur piloted the first flight in a powered heavier-than-air craft on the 300th anniversary of the first importation of Canadian beaver skins at La Rochelle, an event as significant for commerce in its day as flight would be later on. On another December 16, in 1951, an airliner crashed into the Elizabeth River in New Jersey killing 56 people, and 134 were killed in a mid-air collision over New York City in 1960 on yet another December 16.

These crashes might have been prevented had aviators been able to use the five patented systems for algorithms now employed in aircraft tracking systems to avoid collisions. Their inventor, Kathryn Yearra, was born in the fortieth anniversary year of the Kitty Hawk flights, and only three letters differentiate her surname from Chuck's. There was no difference at all in the instance of Jeana Yeager: with Richard Rutan she completed a non-stop around-the-world flight without refueling, on December 23, 1986. Their time was 9 days 3 minutes and 44 seconds, or a total of 777,824 seconds, the arithmetic sum of which is 35; and in the thirty-fifth year of the twentieth century Wiley Post died, having completed the first round-the-world flight in 1933 coincident with the premiere of the film *King Kong*. When he crashed in Alaska, Will Rogers went with him. William Penn Adair Rogers, as God knew him, launched his career on a national scale when he joined the Ziegfeld Follies, at the age of thirty-five.

"Yeager" means "hunter" in German, and also means "fighter plane" in popular German usage. An early German

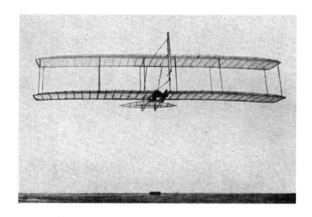

fighter shot down Theodore Roosevelt's son Quentin over Chateau-Thierry on Bastille Day in 1918. Chuck Yeager was a fighter pilot in World War II, flying a B-51 Mustang. Fifty years and one day after Yeager's jet broke the sound barrier, an automobile broke the barrier, and both used Rolls Royce engines.

Jet propulsion flying is a practical application of Isaac Newton's third law of motion. That great but anxious genius (as a youth he threatened to burn his mother and stepfather alive) was born in 1727. Two hundred years later, on May 21, Chuck "Charles" Lindbergh landed at Le Bourget. There was certainly nothing mean or furtive about the celebrations on that occasion. Indeed, they distracted the public from noticing a remarkable coincidence: on the 21st day of May in 1878, in Hammondsport, New York, Glenn H. Curtiss, inventor of the hydroplane, was born. It was his invention of the aileron that enabled the Wright brothers to get off the ground.

On the day before Chuck Yeager's first supersonic flight, he fell off a horse and broke a rib. He went on to break the sound barrier unscathed by the jet propulsion, although he was in searing pain from the horse propulsion. There was a certain historical poetry in that: Hernando de Soto, returning from Oklahoma, fell off his horse in a coma and died at the mouth of the Arkansas River in 1542, exactly a century before the birth of Newton. Quite more astonishingly, this took place on May 21, the date of Lindbergh's triumph 385 years later. The irony of Yeager's horse accident was compounded in 1999 on July 8 when Charles "Pete" Conrad, having walked on the moon during the Apollo 12 voyage in 1969, died at the age of 69 in a motorcycle crash.

No quality of rocket machinery can distract us from the elegance and strength of the horses that carried the human race to the heights of civilization. However fast man flies, he will brag of it in horsepower. Pegasus lives. And let us remember: in mythological accounts, all poetic imagination sprang from the fountain of Hippocrene which first flowed at a touch from the hoof of the flying horse. Imaginative interpreters may read a clandestine prophecy of the aeroplane into the poetry of Samuel Butler, who rode horses:

> For, those that fly, may fly again,
> Which he can never do that's slain.

And Butler, coincidentally, was born three hundred years before the death of Wilbur Wright.

ARMA VIRUMQUE

By an instinct common to all youth who have not had pacifism violently hammered into them, the inventive child will turn any toy into a weapon. War is in the blood and among the sons of Cain; every cradle is Crécy. In his nursery of toy soldiers the typical toddler thinks his playpen is Marathon and his playground Zama. It is an affront to reality and a betrayal of psychology to keep these children, or their parents, ignorant of military history. "I didn't raise my son to be a soldier" may be the song of many mothers but not of Mother Nature. It is the good man, said Harry the King, who shall teach his son the story of the battle.

As combat has been in the blood since the second human generation, soldiers form a long parade of coincidences. A prime example of the particular form of coincidence known as isochronism looms from the mists of the court of Aldfrith. From 786 to 796 he reigned over the British kingdom of Lindsey, bringing prosperity and justice to his people, if we are to believe the scraps left by his official court bard. One thousand years later, an isochronic decade (1786–1796) separated the British refusal to surrender their fort at Detroit and its capture by Captain Moses Porter.

Hardly less impressive is the concordance of the daring Danish raid on the holy island of Iona in 818 and the construction of the first Danish steamship in 1818 as the noble Polish general and friend of America, Kosciuszko, was dying. These subtle coincidences have been ignored by most of the world, but not so the blatant events of 1066, for Halley's Comet (not of course called that back then) became visible over England in January, and those who read great moment in syzygies and other astronomical coincidences suspected that something cataclysmic was about to unfold. They were proved right, for not many events have altered the affairs of men on this earthly orb as did the Norman Conquest.

Cromwell's dramatic victories at Dunbar in 1650 and Worcester in 1651 and his own death in 1658 took place on the third of September. Correlations, synechdoches and consiliences rattled the Battle of the Boyne in Ireland on July 1, 1690. The Catholic army of James II had Protestant mercenaries from Prussia, and the Protestant Orange army had numbers of Catholic mercenaries by way of the French, although the rumor that the Orangemen were backed financially by the dying Pope Innocent XI (Benedetto Odescalchi) has little evidence. Pope Alexander VIII (Pietro [Vito] Ottoboni) continued with a more conciliatory tone his predecessor's policies, which were motivated by an animus against Louis XIV. Thus when a painting of the battle hanging in the Stormont in Belfast was cleaned not long ago, all were surprised to behold an image of the pope in the clouds blessing William of Orange, and the painting was removed altogether. In some vague way, this anticipated Pope Leo XIII's support of the British government against Irish insurrectionists in 1888. On the fatal day at Oldbridge by the Boyne, James II got a violent nosebleed right at the highest pitch of the battle and had to withdraw from the field. Despite his faults, he was an excellent military commander and could have won the day. The king's nosebleed is like the storm that wrecked the Spanish Armada: de-

pending on whose side one stood, it was either blessed providence or tragic coincidence.

Two short years before the death of Kosciuszko, Simon Bolivar sailed back to Latin America from Haitian exile and began his maneuver toward New Granada (*id est* Colombia) unaware that Jose de San Martin, the Argentine general, had begun his own march on Chile and, later, Peru. This unpremeditated pincer effect, thanks to the extraordinary coincidence, was a seminal factor in Bolivar's victories eight years later in Junin and Ayacucho, and shaped the ultimate challenge to Spanish rule on the southern continent.

On the northern continent, the "Bonus Army" of veterans in Washington, D.C. which disbanded on July 28, 1932, was dispersed by Federal troops under the command of Douglas MacArthur. President Hoover's instruction that there be no gunfire was ignored putatively by MacArthur on the grounds that he would not take orders from a civilian. In 1951 a contretemps coincidental in some details led to Truman relieving MacArthur of his command in Korea. MacArthur's aide-de-camp during the Bonus March was the forty-two-year-old Major Dwight Eisenhower. MacArthur died, or faded away as he would have it, on the two thousandth anniversary of the expulsion of Lepidus from the second Roman triumvirate.

I am not sure what we are to conclude from this review of arms and men, but it is never amiss to conjure up the victor of Waterloo in his celebrated dispatch of June, 1815: "Nothing except a battle lost can be half so melancholy as a battle won." William Tecumseh Sherman, having graduated from West Point in the year that the capital of New Zealand was named for the Iron Duke, agreed as he surveyed the carnage at Shiloh: "The scenes on this field would have cured anybody of war." Some celestial symposium made up of all the generals from Alexander the Great to George Patton, who did not make the distinction, would be either the jolliest of fetes or a pitched battle, but overwhelming odds are that they would be unanimous with Wellington's motion.

MEDICINE ON THE MARCH

AMONG THE BENEFACTIONS OF CRUEL WARS HAS BEEN the promotion of medical science. The Hyksos invasion of Egypt advertised the curative properties of senna, as the Inca wars promoted cinchone and quinine. We could ask rhetorically: Would we know today about *nux vomica* had it not been for Chandragupta's army? Robert Koch discovered the cholera bacillus during the German campaign in Egypt in 1884; and had there been no World War, Alexis Carrel might never have developed antiseptic treatment of infected wounds in 1915. Without the Spanish American War, yellow fever would have ravaged Havana and all the tropics much longer. And all that we read in William Harvey's Lumleian Lectures on blood circulation really only quicken our pulse when we realize that this quiet student of Fabricius and Galileo waved the banner for his king on the blood-soaked fields of Edge Hill.

Today rational man need raise no altars to Aesculapius and Chiron when he can build sanitary hospitals in tribute to the military martyrs Jesse Lazear and Major Walter Reed. Nor need we invoke the mythic shade of Hygeia when we can bless the shimmering lights of Clara Barton and Florence Nightingale who, coincidentally, had almost exactly coterminous lives (1821–1912 and 1820–1910). Wistfully, the bacteriologist Aristides Agramonte, military colleague of Lazear and Reed, became secretary of public health in Cuba on the tenth anniversary of Nightingale's death.

It is hard to imagine how anyone could be bored with life when the history of military medicine lies begging to be read. Its scintillating pages can stir the most saturnine pulse, and its radiant paladins can enflame the most slothful of this world's men. Children will easily become disappointed and cynical if the heroes proposed to them are only lumpish rock stars and prosaic professional athletes; they will rejoice with a lifelong contentment if their role models are true paragons like the father of military medicine, Sir John Pringle (1707–1782), who effectively controlled dysentery in the Lowlands. Adolescents could have no better champion than the father of naval hygiene, James Lind (1716–1794), who instituted delousing. Lind designed hospital ships and prescribed citrus to prevent scurvy among sailors, giving rise to the racial pejorative "limey." Captain Cook's officers refused to eat the limes, perhaps ironically so in view of their indiscriminate eagerness for haggis. The first haggis eaten in New Zealand was served up by the appropriately named Captain Cook on his ship *Endeavour* to celebrate the birthday of a Scottish officer on March 9, 1790. Such abuse of nutrition motivated the United States Army surgeon William Beaumont to advance palliatives for gastric indigestion. He died in 1853, which is the same arithmetic sum as 1790 and is also the year of Walter Reed's birth. Medical

improvements made navy life more attractive to those of gentle breeding. The navy had not always had that appeal, and thus we read in Macaulay's *History of England*: "There were gentlemen and there were seamen in the navy of Charles the Second. But the seamen were not gentlemen; and the gentlemen were not seamen."

Gustavus Brown, the Surgeon General of the Revolutionary Army, and James Cralk had the honor of tending George Washington at Mount Vernon in 1799. Although the two Scotsmen were highly trained physicians, the General died from a suppurative inflamation of the tonsils. George Washington and porphyritic George III suffered alike from Bell's palsy, named for another Scot, Sir Charles Bell, father of modern treatment for the central nervous system. Unlike the Scots, the Welsh, as at Agincourt for example, tended to rely solely on the preventative and curative powers of the leak. The absurdity of this did not thwart its popularity among their tribes.

Skipping over a few wars, we come to the Civil War, in which served a native of Schwersenz, Simon Baruch, the most famous Jewish hydrotherapist in the Confederate Army. He fathered the revered Bernard in 1870 and eighteen years later performed the first appendectomy in America. Only six years before that historic surgery, on the centenary of Sir John

Pringle's death, the international press celebrated the May-December marriage of William Lehman Ashmead-Bartlett of Brooklyn and Baroness Angela Burdett-Coutts of London. Ashmead-Bartlett was 30 and Burdett-Coutts was 67. The baroness was heiress to a vast banking fortune which she devoted to philanthropic works. Having emigrated to England, Ashmead-Bartlett extended these works to the reform of medical services in the British Army. The father of Burdett-Coutts, Sir Francis Burdett had led a national campaign to abolish flogging in the army, and the elder brother of Ashmead-Bartlett, Sir Ellis, was a field observer in the Boer War and author of *The Battlefields of Thessaly*.

These valorous figures knew that wars are ennobled only when fought in self-defense to promote peace and justice. Some social analysts less familiar with the history of wars speak of peace and justice in flaccid tones that tend to pacifism and legalism which are not the formula for invention. In more peaceful times, the NASA space program has studied the effects of weightlessness on animals, but I can imagine this only being useful to people who raise pets at high altitudes. I certainly would not make a case for war, but in war the effort is to live, while in peace it is merely to live longer. Wars do have internal motions which make medical progress inevitable. This always is the case where not to advance is to retreat.

MOSES AND THE MUSES

THE ANGLO-IRISH CRITIC ROBERT WILSON LYND observed that only in literature does coincidence seem unnatural. Thus the literary Detection Club, whose members included Dorothy Sayers and Agatha Christie and G. K. Chesterton, denied their fictitious sleuths access to coincidences, along with divine revelation, feminine intuition, mumbo-jumbo, jiggery-pokery, and acts of God. By any parallel logic, synchronicity and other forms of coincidence are not unnatural in the lives of literary authors themselves. I should list only a few compelling examples.

Pindar is known to us today as the Dircaean Swan because he was born about 522 B.C. in Boeotia near the fountain of Dircaea; and swans were sacred to Apollo the father of the Muses. But the humidity of Boeotia made it synonymous with plodding prosaicness. So even now a teacher may insult a dunce with the old Roman aphorism: "Boeotum in crasso jurares aere natum" which almost translates itself: "You'd swear he was born in the thick air of Boeotia." In the House of

Commons, the Irish national leader Daniel O'Connell accused Disraeli of thickness, brazenly using "Jewish" as an equivalent for "Boeotian." Disraeli, the Judaean Swan, rose from his bench and declared to the son of Eire: "I am indeed a Jew. And when the right honourable member's ancestors were savages on an uncharted island, mine were priests in the Temple of Solomon." By this time, Disraeli had succumbed to the rarefied seductions of the Church of England, but this did not completely erase his interest in revealed religion. As the grandson of a true merchant of Venice, perhaps Disraeli's information of the Mosaic Pentateuch influenced his own cadences. Whole passages of his novel *Lothair* seem written from rabbinic chant. "Dizzy" became leader of the House of Commons fittingly on the 300th anniversary of the death of Oliver Cromwell from tertian ague. I say fittingly because Cromwell, a man not without arbitrary prejudices, was a hero to the Jews for having bid them return from exile on the Continent.

Hebrew is God's own language just as, according to Shakespeare's Hotspur, the Devil speaks Welsh. But no human race has a copyright on Hebrew. The seventeenth-century professor of Hebrew at the Roman College was Emil Gustav Hirsch, a Jesuit who, having written at length on the etymology of the Hebrew metaphors for light, coincidentally invented the magic lantern. In the nineteenth century, the professor of Hebrew at the General Theological Seminary in New York City, the Episcopal clergyman Clement Clarke Moore, wrote the ballad "'Twas the Night Before Christmas", which was published anonymously in the Troy (New York) *Sentinel* on December 23, 1823, in which year O'Connell started the Catholic Association in Ireland.

Czech was declared the official language of Bohemia on the two hundredth anniversary of the burning of John Huss, who used poetic hymnody to spread his religious views. Most appropriate, then, was the election of the poet Vaçlev Havel as president of the Czech Republic after the recent "Velvet Revolution." More than one coincidence obtained in Scotland at the apogee of Czech letters. In 1615, Mary Cunningham died on the night before her wedding to William Drummond, the royalist poet who had reservations about the succession of the Elector Palatine, Frederic, in Bohemia. His bride's death makes moving reading of his cancelled epithalamium, and Drummond himself died in tears in the year of his King Charles's execution. Drummond was born in 1585 just as Jan Blahoslav was publishing the Kralicka Bible in Prague and the Spanish were raising their siege of Antwerp after fourteen months: exactly the length of Cardinal Richelieu's siege of La Rochelle in 1628. As sieges go, this isochronism is matched by the Turkish siege of Kut-al-Amara ending in 1916 and the Russian-Rumanian siege of Plevne of 1877, both lasting 144 days. These events occasioned poetry so freighted with unfettered lugubriousness that it failed to capture popular imagination—although it has a modern variant in the repertoires of Hank Williams and Willie Nelson.

Poetry has always made potent politics, from the days blind Homer chanted to the Ionian winds. I trust I am not alone in considering José Pereira da Graça Aranha the Paul Claudel of Brazil. Both poets were born in 1868 and both were politically engaged diplomats. This is to be remembered when the daunting and dismaying modern taste for free verse has enlarged the poets' circle to include antinomian beatniks and habitués of tango palaces. Alexander Pope complained of free verse in the *Prologue to the Satires*: "It is not Poetry, but prose run mad." The twentieth century has been the anthropological equivalent of free verse. We might say that the modern age was not civilization, but existence run mad; and that modernism itself was not philosophy, but facts run mad. Consequently, the Nobel Prize for Literature has become an exercise in the inconsequential trivia which all of us viscerally scorn. The philosophical template for literary exposition is in pieces. Time, however, is a prolific poet with a scythe for a pen. For proof one need only consult this fabulous coincidence: Alexander Pope died on the 1000th anniversary of the death of the Umayyad caliph and amateur poet Walid II, predecessor to Yazid III whose death would have excited the suspicions of the abovementioned Detection Club.

MALICIOUS ANIMAL MAGNETISM

THE FORMER MAYOR MARION BARRY SAID OF CONDI-tions in Washington, D.C. that "the crime rate isn't so bad if you don't count murder." This was an awkward account of the situation in our nation's capital, especially so since the Mayor personally has increased the crime rate. By the encoded logic of its own illogic, any atomistic denial of reality must ultimately refuse to acknowledge death. For instance, as part of its denial of materiality, Mrs. Mary Baker Eddy's sect of Christian Science claims that no one dies. On the death of Mrs. Eddy's third hus-band Asa Gilbert Eddy in 1882, which coincided with the elec-tion of Maximo Santos as president of Uruguay, she tried to surmount this threat to her Manichaean dualism by explaining that he had "passed on" as a result of malicious animal magnet-ism metaphysically induced.

The better classical philosophers rejected surreal cheeriness, even to the point of pessimism, like Heracleitus (c.537–c.475 B.C.), notorious as "the weeper" for his dismal philosophy of all things being impermanent. "All is flux, nothing is stationary."

That, at least, is how Aristotle rendered him in *De Caelo* and Aristotle was very deft indeed at rendering philosophers. By no slight coincidence, Heracleitus was also the name of the friend for whom Callimachus in Halicarnassus wrote his melancholy panegyric almost three hundred years before Christ wept true tears of heaven for Lazarus. This coincidence of Heracleituses continues to cause confusion right up to our own day.

In a Franciscan spirit, denial of death yields to a hope surpassing stoical acceptance. Then many bewildering mortuary coincidences amuse in a positive and kindly way which pole vaults over irony. It would be in bad taste to express satisfaction at the sudden death of the heretic Arius, but it is gratifying that providence pushed his eject button in Constantinople in 336 A.D. on the very day before the Emperor intended to mock the Church by restoring him to communion. A will-'o-the-wisp kind of justice tempered by mercy had modern display when that hammer of religion, Nikita Khrushchev, was buried in Moscow in a convent cemetery, of all places. In a secular vein, there was a parallel retribution in the instance of Aaron Burr, slayer of Alexander Hamilton in a duel on the heights of Weehawken, New Jersey: he rejoiced unduly in 1807 when on September 14, his "happy day", he was acquitted of a misdemeanor charge related to a previous indictment, for in 1836 he died on September 14.

Birth and death contended in stellar synchronicity for Henry Cabot Lodge and Samuel Gompers. Two men could hardly have been more unlike in earthly estate than the Boston Brahmin and the president of the American Federation of Labor. Unlike, that is, except in cradle and tomb, for they were born in 1850 and died in 1924. Another labor leader, James

"Jimmy" Hoffa, head of the Teamsters Union, was officially declared missing on the centenary of the death of Andrew "Andy" Johnson at Carter's Station in Tennessee on July 31, 1875. The very different personality, King Leopold of the Belgians, died on holiday in Cannes exactly one year after he had informed his niece, Queen Victoria, of the death of her highland servant John Brown. Among the royals, Henry VIII and his children Edward VI, Mary, and Elizabeth all died on Tuesdays.

To the point of irony are the joint deaths in 1910 of the aforementioned Mary Baker Eddy, and William James, author of *The Will to Believe and Other Essays* and *The Varieties of Religious Experience*, neither of which volumes seems to have been Mrs. Eddy's beach reading. Nor can we imagine Mrs. Eddy having recourse to the studies of the heteroclitic Andrea Vesalius who used a skeleton to illustrate anatomy lectures at the University of Basel in 1546, during which time Martin Luther died and the Schmalkaldic War began. Vesalius made a pilgrimage to the Holy Land to commute the death sentence imposed on him by the Inquisition for dissecting corpses and promptly died. The skeleton still is displayed in Basel.

According to Suetonius, Vespasian's dying words in 79 A.D. were: "Woe's me. Methinks I'm turning into a god." One would have expected more from the first of the Flavian emperors, but they did not share our high regard for divinity. It was relatively easy for an emperor to become a god, so they rather lowered the theological currency. As W. S. Gilbert said in *The Gondoliers*: "When every one is somebodee / Then no one's anybody." It is a pedestrian gloss on the First Commandment.

On a more intelligent plane than that of anxious Titus Flavius Sabinus Vespasianus are those whose realism sustains them at life's end "ex umbris et imaginibus in veritatem." It would seem that a higher grace organized for three saints to coincide at the deathbed of Pope Pius IV on December 9 in 1565: Charles Borromeo, Philip Neri, and Michele Ghislieri—the future Pope Pius V. By a brilliance of the same grace, the first native saint of the United States, Elizabeth Bayley Seton, died in the 1821, the year of the dedication in Baltimore of the first cathedral in the nation, which was also the 150th anniversary of the appointment of her ancestor Charles Seton, second earl of Dunfermline, as lord privy seal. On the fiftieth anniversary of her death, her grandson William Seton published his *Romance of the Charter Oak*. And the saintly American Capuchin, Father Solanus Casey, celebrated his first Mass in 1904 on July 31 at 11 a.m. and died in 1957 on July 31 at 11 a.m. Out of the shadows and imaginings into the truth. And there was nothing malicious or animal or magnetic about it.

THE HAPPY FARMER

I SHALL ALWAYS BE GRATEFUL TO THE NEIGHBOR OF MY parents who some years ago gave me a copy of Dryden's translation of Virgil's *Georgics*. Splendid as were the illustrative plates, they could not overwhelm the verses of the laurelled poet whom Cowper, slightly provincially, called the Milton of Rome. The average pedestrian need not haul such a large volume about, for we carry some of Virgil with us daily. Whoever has a one dollar bill will notice inscribed under the little pyramid "NOVUS ORDO SECLORUM" from the *Georgics* along with, over the eyeball, "ANNUIT COEPTIS" from the *Aeneid*. Paranoid personalities with shaky Latin frequently mistranslate the *Georgics* line as a dark prophecy of some sinister contemporary "New World Order." The actual case is rather more basic, for the venerable phrase is from the great poet's ode to farming, and "georgicus" is an adjectival referent to "agricola" which means farmer.

One of our nation's two or three finest presidential Latinists, Herbert Hoover reduced the size of the dollar bill to fit more conveniently in wallets and was accused by demagogues of having devalued it. Franklin Roosevelt did indeed devalue the dollar, but there was little complaint because he did not change the size of the paper. Regularly during breakfast, President Hoover and his wife Lou translated passages from Agricola's *De Re Metallica*. One is unlikely to encounter so edifying a scene in the White House of recent memory. In his one stab at Latin in a speech, Albert Gore translated "E PLURIBUS UNUM" backwards.

The *Metallica* was written by the German scholar George Bauer, born in Glachau in Saxony two years after Columbus discovered America. Celebrated as the "Father of Mineralogy", many tend to overlook his competence as an historian and also as a Catholic apologist in a hostile Protestant environment. His latinized name, Georgius Agricola, is glaringly unsuited for a mineralogist. But equally odd is the way four musicians took Agricola for a professional name: Alexander Ackerman (1446–1506), Martin Sohr (1486–1556) and Johann Friedrich, who were German, and the Dutchman Roelof Huysman (1443–1485). The last was, coincidentally with our theme, a classical scholar as well as a musician, but we may know him best today for his painting which included, appropriately enough, farm scenes. Some consider him the forerunner of Daubigny and greater than Constable, but only because they have confused him with Cornelis Huysmans (1648–1727). They would still be wrong, because the only one of whom such might be said is Huysmans's contemporary, Meindert Hobbema (1638–1709).

The Protestant schismatic Johannes Agricola (originally Schneider) further complicated the Agricola network by applying his energies at Wittenberg to spreading Antinomianism. This dissolute philosophical attitude has nothing to do with

agriculture, although Martin Luther (supported by Melanc-
thon) called Johannes Agricola a spreader of fertilizer, or words
to that effect. This Schneider Agricola was born and died in
the same years that the Sohr Agricola was born and died. Base
as it is to read arcane portents into coincidental dates, he would
be superhuman who could not be fascinated by this: in the year
1548, that Schneider Agricola helped Julius von Pflug
(1499–1564) prepare the "Augsburg Interim", the farmers of
Burma recognized Bayinnaung as their ruler, and Bishop
Michael Agricola published his Finnish translation of the New
Testament.

Von Pflug was the Catholic bishop of Naumburg-Zeitz. As a
humanist, he was thoroughly read in Tacitus. The *Annales* had
shown him the ways of the Julian emperors, as the *Historiae* had
made him intimate with Galba, Otho and chubby Vitellius. In
his irenic outlook, he was influenced by the lay cardinal Gaspar
Contarini who had been born on the fiftieth anniversary of the
birth of Rodolphus (Roelof Huysman) Agricola. And that was,
mirabile dictu, the 1400th anniversary of the death of Tacitus's
father-in-law, the immortal Gnaeus Julius Agricola whom Tacitus so admired that he made him the subject of his *Agricola*, a

book precious to Von Pflug. The sonorous cadences of that beautiful literature are almost totally ignored now. These days it is a safe assumption that many if not most high schools spend more time on driver education than on Tacitus. Inasmuch as he was a soldier and politician, Gnaeus Julius Agricola could be called the Lord Townshend of the Roman Empire for his diligence in promoting crop rotation in Britain as part of the *novus ordo seclorum*. Like Townshend, the second Viscount of Raynham, (1674–1738) in his zeal for cultivating turnips, Agricola's agricultural improvements transformed all of Britain save for southern Cymru, where they were rejected by the dolichocephalic Welsh whose intractable instincts repulsed any innovation in their domestic habits.

In *Gulliver's Travels*, Jonathan Swift supports the opinion that "whoever could make two ears of corn or two blades of grass to grow upon a spot of ground where only one grew before, would deserve better of mankind, and do more essential service to his country than the whole race of politicians put together." On this basis, Gnaeus Julius Agricola justifies himself well (even by the protocols of the Augsburg Interim on justification).

The little catalogue above may resolve the persistent confusion of Gnaeus Julius Agricola with Georgius (Bauer) Agricola, which muddies so many accounts of Herbert Hoover's latinity.

ALL IN HARMONY

A CONFEDERATE SENTRY HEARD THE SOUND OF A VOICE coming from marshland behind the enemy lines. He aimed his rifle at a Union soldier who was singing. The tune was possibly John Bacchus Dykes's "Hollingside", first published in 1861, but already quite well known. More likely, it was "Martyn", which had been composed on horseback in 1834 by a music teacher named, coincidentally if we consider the voice of the marshes, Simeon Buckley Marsh. There is no period recording of it, naturally, since the talking machine had not yet been invented by Edison, who established himself in Menlo Park, New Jersey over the space of a few months from 1875 to 1876 during which time both Dykes and Marsh died, although Marsh was Dykes's senior by twenty-five years. What matters more is that the text was Charles Wesley's hymn "Jesus, Lover of My Soul." And what matters most is that just as the sentry was cocking his gun, his target blithely began the line "Cover my defenseless head / With the shadow of thy wing." Their eyes met, the gun was lowered, the parlous moment passed, and each went his way. After the war, the Confederate veteran heard the same voice singing the same hymn on a Potomac River steamer—the

Union soldier was now a preacher leading some sort of revival meeting on the deck. The two veterans embraced and joy festooned their peace. This was one of those harmonious coincidences which gives a particularly lush timbre to the history of hymnody.

Sometime around 1680 in Southampton, England, a little boy saw a mouse going up a bell rope by the fireplace during family prayers and cried out with precocious spontaneity: "There was a mouse for want of stairs ran up a rope to say his prayers." His father, a severe man, was about to cane him for irreverence when the youth pleaded: "O Father, Father, pity take, And I will no more verses make." It is perhaps not a coincidence that young Isaac Watts, the beardless bard, went on to become the father of English hymnody. But there is the undoubted coincidence of the last day in the life of Henry Francis Lyte, author of "Praise my soul, the King of heaven" and "Abide with me".

A Celt of eclectic erudition, Lyte was born in Scotland in

1793 and studied at Trinity College, Dublin and thrice received the English Poetry prize there. Hymn writing took up no small part of his tenure as a perpetual curate of Lower Brixham in Devon where one of his pupils in the vicarage school was the future Lord Salisbury. Tubercular, Lyte sought relief on the French Riviera and died in a hotel in Nice on November 20, 1847, the very day that the Mexican government decided to discuss peace with the United States. As he was prepared to die, but not as a Roman Catholic, he prayed for the ministrations of a clergyman of the Church of England and blessed providence upon learning that there was one staying in his hotel. So the Archdeacon of Chichester gave him the ministration of the dying according to the rites of the Church of England, as Lyte recited for his last time his own verse: "Hold thou thy cross before my closing eyes."

It was not a rare coincidence to find an English archdeacon choosing the Riviera for his retreat, but it was ironic that this particular one was Henry Edward Manning, who became the only Prince of the Holy Roman Church to be buried with his late wife's Book of Common Prayer. "Abide with me" attained worldwide popularity partly through its promotion by the contralto Dame Clara Butt, who sang it last in 1936, dying on the golden anniversary of Lord Salisbury's resumption of the Premiership.

Morbidity reached extravagant heights with the Rector of Guildford in England, John Monsell. His parish was strapped for cash. In order to raise money for roof repairs on the Church of St. Nicholas, he wrote a hymn which included the nervous stanza:

> Dear body thou and I must part
> Thy busy head, thy throbbing heart
> Must cease to work, must cease to play
> For me at no far distant day.

It was just the sort of hymn that sold back then like hot-cakes, and enough money was raised for the roof. The Rev. Mr. Monsell climbed a ladder to inspect the repairs, fell off and fatally parted from his body. This was on August 9, 1875, to the very day the twenty-fifth anniversary of the approval of the boundary between Texas and New Mexico.

Another vicar, John Ellerton of Barnes, wrote the evening hymn "The day thou gavest, Lord, is ended." Queen Victoria commanded that it be sung at her Diamond Jubilee service in St. Paul's Cathedral, when the Archbishop of Canterbury, and father of the minor hymnographer Robert Hugh Benson, accommodated those who wanted him in a mitre and those who did not by wearing a small gold cap. Victoria much admired her own Albert's spiritual anthems. On October 21, 1998 the Albert Memorial was unveiled after a restoration costing $18.7 million dollars, the same arithmetic sum as the 169 statues on its lower frieze. Perhaps no more coincidentally than the daily rising and setting of the sun, the hymn sung at the Jubilee apogee of empire was sung in 1997 at the final ceremony as Hong Kong was returned to the Chinese.

ARTS AND SCIENCES

DIFFERENT HEMISPHERES OF THE BRAIN GOVERN THE propensity for intuitive artistry and inductive science. Extreme atrophy of one of the lobes can cause exaggerated aestheticism or nerdish scientism. Acute distinctions between the arts and sciences are artificial and unscientific. One dead lobe creates the National Endowment for the Arts and another dead one creates Planned Parenthood.

The ancients did not distinguish between parts of the brain. In cultural emoluments, Athens and Sparta were more alike than San Francisco and Los Angeles. There are the examples of art and engineering combined in Leonardo and Michelangelo and, more recently, Pierre Duhem. The career of Duhem is particularly interesting from our purview, for on the artistic side he was born in the year of John James Audubon's death and on the scientific side he died in the year of the death of Percival Lowell. Moreover, Audubon was as much a scientist as he was an artist and Lowell was as much an artist as he was a scientist, making the very heavens his canvass. Rubens may have been more of a polymath than any of them. He certainly was a better diplomat, an official one to Spain and England. He probably

also developed the assembly-line, though this is considered suspect in an artist. His adroitness in combining aestheticism and pragmatism later got the goat of Ruskin, while it fascinated Taine: "Rubens mounted to Olympus with his heels weighted by quintals of Dutch cheese." Walter Savage Landor saw nothing admirable in such a hybrid, and really cut Wordsworth: "He keeps one eye on a daffodil and the other on a canal-share." But Wordsworth (remark the coincidence of his name and his art) was a poet who painted badly, not to mention that he often wrote very badly, and for the sake of expediency I want to confine epigrams here to painters.

The most obvious mix of art and science is in the concrete world of architecture. Great painters would be builders, and vice versa. That was so of Vitruvius. It was also true of Antonio Canaletto. His nephew, Bernardo Bellotto, drew cityscapes of Warsaw and Dresden from architectural sketches whose detail surpassed that of Canaletto's scenes of Venice and London. Coincidence made Bellotto something of a storm petrel: he happened to sketch two of the cities that would be most devastated in World War II. The silver lining to this jinx is that Bellotto's pictures furnished primary data for the reconstruction of the cities when the original blueprints had all been destroyed.

In 1792, Benjamin West of Pennsylvania succeeded Sir Joshua Reynolds as president of the Royal Academy, which had been founded in 1768 as the coincidentally named mathematician Benjamin West of Massachusetts was publishing his *Boston Alamanc*, but it cannot be said that the former was much of a scientist. However, Samuel F. B. Morse became first president of the National Academy of Design and was commissioned to do some paintings in Italy. He invented the telegraph in his painting studio in Washington Square as professor of art at New York University. Scientific acumen does not guarantee a dispassionate intelligence of daily affairs. Morse became one of the most notorious anti-Catholic pope-bashers as the result of having had his hat knocked off by a papal zouave when he was watching Pope Pius VII go by.

Morse finally got a patent for the telegraph in 1840, having filed a caveat three years earlier. In 1856, he went abroad to prepare the laying of the Atlantic cable. At the time, the chief examiner of the U.S. Patent Office was Titian Ramsey Peale of America's most famous art dynasty before the Wyeths. His father Charles had opened a combination art gallery and natural history museum on the second floor of what we now call Independence Hall. Young Peale accompanied Major Long's expedition to the Upper Missouri in 1819, producing drawings second in scientific importance only to those of Audubon, whose first volume of *The Birds of America* was released to the public as Morse was scuffling with the pope's guard.

Whistler failed chemistry at West Point long before he painted his mother. It is also true, however, that in 1867, as he was repudiating Courbet's realism, a son was conceived by the wife of the marine and landscape painter William Trost Richard. This nascent Theodore William Richards would win the Nobel Prize for Chemistry in 1914 on the eightieth anniversary of Whistler's birth. Such an association inescapably conjures up the long line of Harveys: for while there was not much physical science in Eli Harvey, who sculpted a gorilla for the New York Geological Society, his death in 1957 marked the tercentenary of the death of William Harvey, whose studies of blood circulation have somewhat overshadowed his valuable investigation of generation among apes.

Philosophy boils down to the relationship between the "pulcher" and the "utile." Is beauty that which is useful, or is the useful that which is beautiful? Only humans ask the question. Angels know the answer, and animals have no Latin. Humans ask it because they are artists and scientists. Phidias was accused of blasphemy for carving his own image on Athena's shield. He was a pagan precursor of Michelangelo carving his name on the Pieta and of Pinturicchio painting his name on one of the arrows in St. Sebastian. Each signature declared that man is not a creator of gods but is created in such a way that he can know that he is created. It is almost the definition of art to call it the declaration of creatureliness. It is not blasphemous to put our signature on beauty or to boast of invention, but to make an ugly thing and call it beautiful and to make a useless thing and call it useful is a very modern form of blasphemy known as ideology.

TABLE TALK

THE POET AND CRITIC MATTHEW ARNOLD (1822–1888)
arrived in New York on the Cunarder "Servia" in October of
1883 to begin a lecture tour. The Mahdi was rampant in Egypt,
the Triple Alliance was sealed, and a Bulgarian plot to kidnap
Prince Alexander of Battenburg had just been foiled. Quieter
than these events, but far more captivating to our imagination,
is the extraordinary coincidence of Arnold boarding a train to
Binghamton and realizing that the passenger seated next
to him was the "Hoosier Poet" James Whitcomb Riley
(1849–1916). Who has soul so dead that he would not long to
have been a fly on the wall of the dining car on that day? Riley
is enshrined in an Ionic tomb on a promontory of Indianapolis
above the simpler grave of President Benjamin Harrison. Benjamin's illustrious grandfather William Henry died of pneumonia in the White House on April 4 in 1841, coincident with
the appointment of Arnold's laurelled father Thomas to the
Regius professorship of history in Oxford during the pontificate
of the Cappellari-Colomba Pope Gregory XVI, who condemned railways. This Pope Gregory, whose antipathy to the
locomotive was inconsistent with his promotion of steamboat

traffic at Ostia, spoke to no one during his meals and sat at a separate table when dining with relatives.

Not all railway encounters are so happy for the arts as that of 1883. In 1960, Mick Jagger and Keith Richards met on a train for the first time in ten years, having attended primary school together, and their chat led to the formation of the choral group known as the "Rolling Stones." The records of Arnold's table talk with Riley are sparse. For wit, it could have surpassed the celebrated salon of Madame Recamier, who died as Riley was being born. She had a sofa named after her and died on the same day and month in 1849 as the day and month in 1920 when the Chicago entrepreneur Alphonse "Al" Capone shot James "Big Jim" Colosimo. None of Mr. Capone's intimate circle was a gifted conversationalist. On at least one occasion, the snappish Capone approached a man who was seated at table and bashed him to Hades with a baseball bat.

Capone's gesture was no substitute for wit, but even wit can be hurtful in table conversation. Social history is enlivened time and again by deipnosophistic kerfuffles. And a kerfuffle is, need we say, a tart exchange, a fluttery squabble. At a dinner party in London, the writer Arnold Bennett (1867–1931) attempted to start a conversation by complaining about the hanging of some pictures in the National Gallery. An icy silence was broken by the announcement that the guest to whom he was speaking was W. G. Constable, the Gallery's assistant director. More entertaining was an incident in a dining room that must have witnessed many literary jousts more kinetic than the rehearsed banter at the fabled Algonquin Hotel round table in New York. During a luncheon at the London firm of Faber and Faber when T. S. Eliot was working there, something agitated the tone of the conversation. We do not know what it was, but it gave birth to an heroic example of the literary coincidence known as a palindrome: one of the table guests, an American publisher, left the table muttering, "Was it Eliot's toilet I saw?" One likes to think that it was an unrehearsed spark of intimacy with the Muse. Alfonse "Al" Capone never spoke thus.

In 1953, Winston Churchill hosted a dinner at No. 10 Downing Street for the Italian Prime Minister, Alcide De Gasperi. The gentleman seated across from Madame De Gasperi happened to be Field Marshall Harold Rupert Alexander, first Earl of Tunis. Unaware that two years earlier Alexander had commanded the invasion of Sicily in June and the Italian coast in September, and had been Commander in Chief of the allied forces in Italy from 1944 to 1945, Madame De

Gasperi asked him politely in halting English: "Do you know Italy?" "Yes, Ma'am. I do, a bit." Faces froze as she persisted: "Where have you been in Italy?" "Oh, up and down, don't you know, up and down." After brandy, perhaps by another mere coincidence, Churchill suffered a stroke which was long kept secret, but from which he never fully recovered. The Italian Prime Minister died the following year. This melancholy note notwithstanding, there is a gratifying symmetry about that dining room, for only a few years earlier Chamberlain and von Ribbentrop exchanged condescending remarks about Churchill, who was in political disfavor and was seated at the far end of the table. Churchill felt the slight, but resourcefully enjoyed his own conversation within himself.

Drones make a policy of not discussing politics and religion at table. This was raised to a high etiquette by Thomas Sheridan. Dr. Johnson, the patron saint of table talk, said of him: "Sherry is dull, naturally dull; but must have taken him a great deal of pains to become what we now see of him. Such an excess of stupidity, sir, is not in Nature." If intelligent minds are present at table, attempts to be anodyne will not direct conversation inevitably in the ways of peace. Meals that are good for the mind are not certain to be good for the digestion. Samuel Butler laid down that a hen is only an egg's way of making another egg, and it could likewise be said that a dinner is only the conversationalist's way of making more conversation. But the art of conversation is practically nonexistent these days, and wit is dead. If mind and heart are not in the conversation, it is well to be excused from the supper altogether. There is a two-thousand-year-old precedent for that.

A SONG OF INDIA

FACING ME EVERY MORNING ON THE WALL OF THE ROOM where I take my coffee and cast a cold eye on the *New York Times* is a small engraving of Edward Law, the first baron Ellenborough (1750–1818). What a remarkable stretch his life spanned, born in the year of the Lisbon earthquake and dying as Illinois was admitted to the Union. By pure coincidence, he hangs next to an engraving of Clement XII, the Corsini pope who went blind in the year that Lord Ellenborough's father began teaching metaphysics at Cambridge. I have made Ellenborough an icon on my wall because his brother Thomas, seventh son of the Anglican Bishop of Carlisle, came to the United States in the year of Bernadotte's accession to the Norwegian throne and married Martha Washington's daughter, Anne Custis. In a coincidence almost psychedelic in its improbability, he became a principle organizer of a national currency for the new nation in the same way that another Law, who was not related, had emigrated from Scotland to issue paper currency for the first bank of France, the Banque Generate, in 1716.

Those who to this day champion the legacy of Chait Singh,

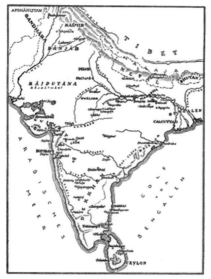

the zamindar of Benares, probably take umbrage at Ellenborough's visage. In 1788 he was made defense counsel at the impeachment of that bad egg Warren Hastings, scourge of the maratha at Maharajpur and looter of the jewels of the begum of Oudh. This meant he had to contend in trial with Burke and Sheridan—no easy task. At the impeachment, Burke said that Hastings "resolved to die in the last dyke of prevarication." But Edward Law (a coincidentally appropriate name for an attorney general and authority on mercantile law) did the work assigned to him, and Hastings was acquitted in 1795. The father dutifully reared his young Edward in the protocols of justice, and the future Earl of Ellenborough did not dishonor his father when he succeeded Lord Auckland as governor general of India in 1841, which coincided with the year that the family of Mehemet Ali became heirs to the pashalik of Egypt. Compounding the Law-law symmetry is this curiosity: Edward Law became governor general precisely one hundred years before the penologist Lewis Lawes, author of *20,000 Years in Sing Sing*, resigned the wardenship of that bleak prison.

The fifty-one year-old earl, grandnephew of Martha Washington, was just and merciful and a very model of manhood. It is nice to think of him as related to Robert E. Lee, through Lee's wife Mary, whose father George Washington Parke Custis was the brother of Thomas Law's wife. Thus Robert E. Lee of the Confederacy was the son-in-law of the brother-in-law of the brother of the first baron Ellenborough, progenitor of a hero of India. True to his name of Law, the legal eagle Edward wrote the home constitution for India. He was not altogether well served by Sir Charles James Napier (named in honor of Charles James Fox, his cousin), whom he put in charge of the simmering war with the testy emirs of Sind in northwest India. Ignoring Ellenborough's orders to be kind, Napier provoked the volatility of the enemy. He annexed all of Sind in 1843 and presented it to the Crown as a *fait accompli* even before the emirs had agreed to accept the conditions of their reduced estate. Sweet death kissed the lips of Napier on the one thousandth anniversary of King Ethelwulf's final triumph over the Danes at Ockley.

There was a bit of Teddy Roosevelt in Napier's blend of exuberance and erudition. One thinks of Roosevelt taking volumes of Norse sagas on his Brazilian expedition and reading *Alice in Wonderland* and *The Federalist* with equal relish in Africa. When Napier captured the city of Miani in central Sind in 1843, he wanted to trumpet his achievement in an encoded message to Ellenborough. But how to do it? Even before the victory was assured he sent a message of one word, one Latin word that is: "Peccavi." It became one of history's most glorious puns, although even effervescent Latin puns are considered verbal coincidences of a low order. It was also an unintended double *double-entendre* because to say "I have sinned" was also to comment on Napier's contempt for Ellenborough's instructions. The only verbal coincidence that approaches it is, coincidentally, also Latin-Indian. Let me explain. Ellenborough was succeeded as governor general by Hardinge, and Hardinge by Dalhousie. Meanwhile, beginning with Sind, annexation followed upon annexation. After battles such as those of Mudki, Firuzshah, Aliwal, and Sobraon, the Punjab was annexed and then Pegu and Oudh. As the taking of Sind was announced with "Peccavi", so the proud message for Lord Dalhousie upon the capture of Oudh was "Vovi": I have vowed.

There are those of us, and they include one who eats his matitudinal toast beneath the gaze of Ellenborough, who suspect that Latin codes are not spontaneously passed around the Pentagon in our day. It is worse to think that English is not well served in those corridors. Even less confidently can we imagine the Oval Office of the White House echoing with Latin iambics and grammatical English. By the intercession of Napier, shriven of any faults he may have committed against the grudge-bearing folk of Maharajpur and Panniar, there may come a day not far distant when the language that Caesar shouted across the Rubicon will better be understood by the littler Caesars on the Potomac. I shall wait for that. *Nil desperandum*. And wait.

POTPOURRI

THERE COMES A TIME TOWARD THE END OF A DINNER
when the crumbs are gathered up. Nicely crafted crumbers are
not uncommon for the purpose. In surveying the vast, yea virtually limitless field of coincidences, inevitably there will be
items that remain like crumbs, but when put together they
make their own loaf of synchrony and concomitance. In gathering these remnants I make no apology for lack of theme, for
their eclectic character is itself their unity and their coincidental nature is their reason.

So they are made precious by being random, diamonds in
the rough if you will, but diamonds nonetheless. The metaphor
is not undue, for diamonds would be worthless were their supply not controlled, and so is it with coincidences. Were all of
them apparent to us, they would be as unremarkable as the air
itself. But each displayed in isolated splendor is a jewel as shining and faceted as the 565-carat Star of India sapphire which
was stolen from the American Museum of Natural History in
New York City on October 29, 1964, coincidentally the day
that, three years later, the laser beam pioneer Charles Hard
Townes would be awarded the Nobel Prize in Physics.

Dates perforce will occasion a little eyebrow-raising. Here is a case in point: in 206 B.C., as the Carthaginians unfeelingly were being expelled from Spain, the Spartans got their due at Mantinea and the Han dynasty was established in China. It may be overstated to call this more than a coincidence, but it would be meaningless to say it was less than a coincidence. You would have to say the same of the unspeakable Japanese attack on Pearl Harbor on the fiftieth anniversary of the invention by James Naismith in Springfield, Massachusetts of something as banal as basketball.

Dates supply the woof and warp of coincidences about the presidency. According to the Census Bureau, the population of the United States attained 200,000,000 on November 20, 1967; little did those diligent bureaucrats seem to appreciate that this was 102 years to the day after the House Judiciary Committee first recommended impeachment proceedings against Andrew Johnson. Collaterally, eleven articles of impeachment were submitted against Johnson on May 16, 1868 and by May 26 the president was acquitted because the Senate's opinion on each article was decided coincidentally by one vote short of a two-thirds majority. And as the Senate was ratifying the United Nations Charter on July 28, 1945, a B-25 crashed into the 79th floor of the Empire State Building. It is also fascinating to observers of the Congress that the eighteenth amendment to the Constitution was ratified in 1919 and the nineteenth amendment was ratified in 1920.

Helen Keller closed her vacant eyes in death on the centenary of President Johnson's acquittal. Among her many benefactions was the promotion of sculpture as a teaching device for the visually impaired. It is therefore moving to the heart and intrigu-

ing to the mind to recall that Keller was the family name of Jean Jacques and his brother Jean Balthasar who cast most of the bronze statues in the royal gardens at Versailles. These have given much enjoyment to the blind, who are not deprived of the sense of touch. Unfortunately, the fountains of Versailles were not as successful. Although they were brilliantly engineered by hydraulic pumps ("Machines de Marley") which functioned from 1682 until 1804, they tended to spout sewage, which particularly offended the compensatory olfactory sensibility of blind people. Each of the Keller brothers was born exactly one hundred years before one of the two treaties of Vienna, those of 1735 and 1738, which so agitated the blind Pope Clement XII.

To this potpourri add a rare condiment: the impeached President Johnson had the same surname as the English adventurer who in 1807 committed fraudulent acts at Tortola and, after conspiring on the London Stock Exchange, was impeached and expelled from the House of Commons in 1814.

In matters of finance, the $25,000,000 paid by the United

States to Colombia as compensation for the loss of Panama was identical to the price paid by the United States to Denmark for its part of the Virgin Islands. In that deliberation, the rapacious exactions of the Colombian generals provoked Theodore Roosevelt to use a pejorative term for people of Spanish extraction. The preliminary negotiations for procuring the Virgin Islands, formally completed in 1916, were begun in 1867 on the centenary of the birth of Theodore's great-grand uncle, Nicholas J. Roosevelt, the inventor of a vertical paddle wheel. He applied for a patent for the wheel in the birth year of Kierkegaard, which is a highly compelling circumstance since the philosopher wrote his *Fear and Trembling* for Regine (Olsen), the daughter of a Danish governor of the Virgin Islands.

How splendid are all these historical shades gliding through the corridors of centuries. He who is not conscious of history, if not dead might as well be. When asked in 1892 at the age of four how he occupied himself during fits of insomnia, little Ronald Knox replied: "I lie awake and think about the past." The same story was told of the boy George Augustus who became King George II, and the correspondence across two centuries is probably fascinating only to this writer among all the billions of people now living, which thing itself is a coincidence.

Index

Index

Bentley, Edmund Clerihew, 16
Berlioz, Hector, 114
Bernacchi, Antonio, 40
Bernacchi, Louis Charles, 40
Bernhardt, Sarah, 30, 126
Bernini, Giovanni Lorenzo, 70
Birdwood, George, 68
Bjornson, Bjornstjerne, 113
Blahoslav, Jan, 181
Blair, Tony, 71
Bligh, William, 152–153
Bluetooth, Henry, 45
Boadicea, Boudicca, 79–80
Bodley, Thomas, 109
Bolivar, Simon, 173
Bonaparte, Napoleon, 107, 147–150
Booth, Edwin, 123
Borromeo, Charles, 186
Boucicault, Dion, 38
Brahmagupta, 82
Breakspeare, Nicholas, 81
Bridges, Robert, 160
Brooke, James, 125
Brooks, Preston S., 38
Brown, John, 34, 131, 185
Bryan, William Jennings, 138
Bryant, William Cullen, 163
Bunsen, Robert Wilhelm, 135
Burdett-Coutts, Angela, 178
Burke, Edmund, 141
Burns, Thomas, 56
Burton, Robert, 99
Bush, George Herbert Walker, 44
Butler, Samuel, 170, 204
Butt, Clara, 193
Byron, Lord, 2, 24, 107

C

Cabanis, Pierre, 27
Caesar, Julius, 91, 96, 164
Caligula, 57
Calvin, John, 50
Cambrensis, Giraldus, 110
Canaletto, Antonio, 197
Cantor, Eddie, 122
Cão, Diogo, 18
Capone, Alphonse "Al", 202–203
Carlyle, Thomas, 27
Carrel, Alexis, 175
Carter, Howard, 102
Carter, James Earl, 45
Casey, Solanus, 186

Chalon, John James, 149
Chamberlain, Neville, 49
Chambers, John Graham, 55
Chaplin, Charlie, 73
Charlemagne, 23
Charles I, 70
Charles III, 31
Charles the Bald, 164
Charles X, 144
Chaucer, Geoffrey, 114
Chauvin, Nicholas, 148
Chesterton, G. K., 179
Chi-jui, Tuan, 90
Child, Julia, 85
Christian, Fletcher, 7, 152
Christian IX, 140
Christian VIII, 140
Christie, Agatha, 179
Churchill, Winston, 11, 129, 165, 203–204
Clay, Henry, 107
Clement III, 110
Clement VI, 83, 85
Clement XII, 205, 211
Cleopatra, 128
Cleveland, Grover, 49
Clinton, Bill, 71
Clinton, DeWitt, 26
Cocteau, Jean, 154
Coel of Caernarfon, 21
Colosimo, James "Big Jim", 202
Connolly, John, 158
Conrad, Charles "Pete", 170
Constable, W. G., 203
Constantine, 12
Constantius, 22
Cooke, Hope, 118
Cooke, Jay, 46
Corbett, James, 55
Corelli, Arcangelo, 152
Cornwallis, Charles, 142
Cortes, Hernando, 95–96
Cory, William Johnson, 62
Cossa, Baldassare, 162
Coste, Dieudonne, 135
Couch, Jonathan, 72
Cralk, James, 177
Cranmer, Thomas, 38
Crawford, Jane Todd, 35
Crémazie, Octave, 163
Cristina, Maria, 118
Cromwell, Oliver, 12, 125, 156, 172, 180
Cruickshank, William, 35

214

Index

Index

George II, 212
George III, 54, 77, 177
George IV, 77
George V, 128
George VI, 49, 103
Gershwin, George, 63
Gershwin, Ira, 63
Ghislieri, Michele, 186
Ghori, Mohammed, 85
Gilbert, W. S., 186
Gladstone, William Ewart, 59–61
Gluck, Barbara, 10
Gluck, Christoph Willibald, 10
Goldwyn, Samuel, 151
Gompers, Samuel, 184
Goodwin, Thomas, 156–157
Gordon, Charles George, 87–88
Gore, Albert, 52, 82, 97, 188
Gramme, Zenobe Theophile, 136
Grant, Ulysses S., 131
Gray, Robert, 138
Gray, Thomas, 105
Gregory XIII, 96
Gregory XVI, 26, 67, 201
Grout, Donald J., 114
Guarneri, Giuseppe, 25
Guillotin, Joseph, 125
Guthrie, Samuel, 33
Gwynedd, Dafydd ab Owain, 110
Gwynn, Nell, 3

H

Hales, Stephen, 73
Hall, Asaph, 53
Hamilton, Alexander, 184
Hamon, Louis, 101
Handel, George Frederic, 114–115
Harrison, Benjamin, 201
Harrison, William Henry, 121, 201
Harvey, Edmund, 152
Harvey, Eli, 198
Harvey, John Martin, 152
Harvey, William, 175, 198
Hastings, Warren, 206
Havel, Vaçlev, 181
Hayden, Charles, 53
Heine, Alice, 154
Helen of Troy, 31
Hellenophile, 53
Hendrix, Jimi, 115
Henry II, 99
Henry V, 76, 96

Henry VIII, 51, 138, 185
Heracleitus, 183
Herbert, George Edward Stanhope Molyneux, 102
Herndon, Hugh, 101
Herostratus, 108
Herschel, Friedrich Wilhelm, 54
Herter, Christian Archibald, 127
Hincks, Edward, 136
Hirsch, Emil, 98
Hirsch, Emil Gustav, 181
Hitchcock, Alfred, 151
Hitler, Adolf, 29
Hoffa, James, 184–185
Holmes, Justice, 12
Holmes, Oliver Wendell, 61
Holyfield, Evander, 55, 58
Homer, 182
Hoover, Herbert, 174, 187–188, 190
Houston, Sam, 49
Howe, Julia Ward, 113
Hughes, John, 49
Hunsaker, Jerome Clarke, 18
Hunter, John, 34
Hunter, William, 34
Huskinsson, William, 8
Huss, John, 181
Huvelin, Abbé, 144
Huxley, Aldous, 124
Huysman, Roelof, 188
Huysmans, Cornelis, 188
Hyatt, Isaiah, 53
Hyatt, John, 53

I

Inge, William Ralph, 66
Ingemann, Bernard Severin, 63
Innocent III, 84
Innocent XI, 172
Irving, Paulus, 126
Irving, Washington, 125

J

Jackson, Andrew, 35
Jackson, Michael, 41
Jackson, Stonewall, 132
Jagger, Mick, 202
James II, 172–173
James III, 158
James, Thomas Potts, 82
James, William, 185
Jarir, 111

Index

Jefferson, Thomas, 44, 122, 139
Jeffries, John, 25
Jenkins, Robert, 127
Jenner, William, 34
Jerome, Jerome Klapka, 11
Joan of Arc, 3, 147
Johansson, Ingemar, 17
John Paul II, 133
John Surratt, 144
John XXII, 83
John XXIII, 68, 70, 83, 162
Johnson, Andrew, 185, 210
Johnson, John "Jack", 56
Johnson, Samuel, 105
Jones, John Paul, 64–65
Joseph II, 142
Josepha, Maria, 3

K

Karageorgevich, Peter, 78
Keene, Laura, 25
Keller, Helen, 210
Keller, Jean Balthasar, 211
Keller, Jean Jacques, 211
Kelly, Grace, 154
Kennedy, John F., 9–10, 124
Khan, Genghis, 100
Khrushchev, Nikita, 184
Kipling, Rudyard, 143–144
Knox, Edmund Arbuthnott, 66
Knox, John, 34, 36
Knox, Ronald, 66, 137, 212
Koch, Robert, 175
Kohl, Helmut, 22
Kyi, Daw Aung San Suu, 101

L

"Lackland", John, 84
Lake, Simon, 82
Lamb, Caroline, 107
Lamb, William, 86
Landor, Walter Savage, 196
Lane, Mills, 55
Lang, Cosmo Gordon, 166
Langhorne, Nancy, 49
Larsen, Don, 91
Laughton, Charles, 51, 152
Law, Edward, 205–206
Law, Thomas, 207
Lawes, Lewis, 206
Lazear, Jesse, 175
Leakey, Colin, 71

Leakey, Mary, 71
Lear, Edward, 106
Leblich, Domingo Badia y, 98
LeClerq, Tanaquil, 126
Lee, Robert E., 131–132, 207
Leishman, William, 34
Leka I, 119
Lenk, Timur, 99
Leo XII, 26, 68
Leo XIII, 94, 173
Leovigildo, 38, 40
Leverrier, Urbain Jean Joseph, 135
Leverrier, Jean Joseph, 54
Lewis, C. S., 62, 124
Liguori, Alphonsus, 41
Lincoln, Abraham, 9–10,
    29, 44, 61, 123–124, 130, 144
Lincoln, Mary Todd, 106
Lincoln, Robert Todd, 123
Lincoln, Willie, 123
Lind, James, 176
Lindbergh, Chuck "Charles", 169–170
Livingston, David, 3, 34
Lockwood, Belva Ann, 54
Lodge, Henry Cabot, 184
Lord Clanricarde, 128
Lord Mountbatten of Burma, 137
Lord Raglan, 134
Lord Salisbury, 193
Louis IV, 83
Louis IX, 159
Louis XII, 138
Louis XIV, 26, 142, 172
Louis XV, 17
Louis XVI, 125, 143, 165
Lowell, Percival, 195
Loyola, St. Ignatius, 3
Luther, Martin, 26, 185, 189
Lynd, Robert Wilson, 179
Lyte, Henry Francis, 192–193

M

MacArthur, Douglas, 174
Macaulay, Thomas Babington, 59, 60, 162, 177
MacDonald, Jeanette, 114
MacGahan, Januarius Aloysius, 77
Mackay, Mary, 152
MacKay, Sandy, 56
Madison, James, 122
Maelzel, Johann Nepomuk, 115
Maitland, Charles, 34
Mallinckrodt, George W., 109

Index

Index

Poe, Edgar Allan, 61, 70
Polk, James Knox, 36, 49, 121
Pope, Alexander, 81, 182
Porter, Moses, 172
Potter, Simeon, 134
Pouishnov, Lev, 117
Pound, Ezra, 105, 106
Poussin, Nicholas, 26
Preston, Rachel D., 98
Priestley, Joseph, 81
Prince Augustus, 3
Pringle, John, 176–178
Prout, William, 135
Pushkin, Aleksandr Sergeevich, 153–154

Q
Qajar, Hamid, 117

R
Rawlinson, 136
Henry Creswicke, 136
Reagan, Ronald, 45, 116
Reed, Walter, 175–176
Reeves, John, 108
Rennie, John, 159
Reynolds, Joshua, 197
Rhinotmetus, Justinian II, 127
Richard II, 49
Richard, William Trost, 198
Richards, Keith, 202
Richards, Theodore William, 198
Ride, Sally K., 82
Riley, James Whitcomb, 201
Robertson, Frederick William, 122
Rogers, Will, 168
Rogers, William Penn Adair, 168
Romulus, 12
Roosevelt, Eleanor, 72
Roosevelt, Franklin, 187
Roosevelt, Nicholas J., 212
Roosevelt, Quentin, 169
Roosevelt, Theodore,
    62, 131, 167, 169, 207, 212
Routh, Martin, 163, 166
Rutan, Richard, 168
Rutherford, Margaret, 153–154
Rutledge, Ann, 61

S
Saltykov, Mikhail Evgrafovich, 11
Sand, George, 69
Santos, Maximo, 183

Saud, Ibn, 30
Saunders, Daniel, 140
Savage, Thomas, 81
Sayers, Dorothy, 179
Sayre, Francis B., 121
Scarlatti, Domenico, 114
Schnitzer, Edward, 3
Schrank, Joseph, 167
Schumann, Paul, 85
Schumann-Heink, Ernestine, 85
Seneca, Lucius Annaeus, 64
Seton, Charles, 186
Seton, Elizabeth Bayley, 186
Seton, William, 186
Shakespeare, William,
    81, 89, 96, 103, 163, 180
Shaw, George Bernard, 135
Shaw, Robert Gould, 118
Sheridan, Thomas, 204
Sherman, William Tecumseh, 174
Shields, Brooke, 120
Sholokhov, Mikhail Alexandrovich, 153
Simpson, James Young, 33
Singh, Chait, 205–206
Sixtus V, 26
Skene, Alexander, 35
Smart, Christopher, 105
Smellie, William, 34
Smith, Sydney, 60
Sohr, Martin, 188
Spencer, Diana, 3
Spencer, Herbert, 163
Squanto, 7, 8
St. Elizabeth of Hungary, 119
St. Elizabeth of Portugal, 119
St. Helena, 21–22
St. Sergius, 127
St. Teresa of Avila, 96
Stanley, Henry Morton, 3
Stowe, Harriet Beecher, 38
Stuart, J. E. B., 131
Sturluson, Snorri, 165
Styles, Thomas, 55, 106
Suetonius, 186
Sumner, Charles, 38
Sweet, Henry, 135
Swift, Jonathan, 53, 190

T
Tacitus, 189–190
Talbot, William Henry Fox, 135
Taylor, Robert Love, 65

219

Index

About the Author

George William Rutler was ordained to the diaconate in Rome by His Eminence William Cardinal Baum in 1980 and received priestly ordination in St. Patrick's Cathedral at the hands of His Eminence Terence Cardinal Cooke in 1981. He has served several New York City congregations including St. Joseph's in Bronxville, Our Lady of Victory in the Wall Street area, and St. Agnes in Manhattan. In 2001 he was appointed by Cardinal Egan as Pastor of the Church of Our Saviour, also in Manhattan. He was a university chaplain for the Archdiocese of New York, and also chaplain to a general hospital and a psychiatric hospital. For ten years he was National Chaplain of Legatus, the organization of Catholic business leaders and their families, engaged in spiritual formation and evangelization. A board member of several schools and colleges, he is also Chaplain of the New York Guild of Catholic Lawyers and has long been associated with the Missionaries of Charity, and other religious orders, as a retreat master. Since 1988 his weekly television program has been broadcast worldwide on EWTN. Father Rutler has lectured and given retreats in many nations, frequently in Ireland and Australia.

Born in 1945 and reared in the Episcopal tradition in New Jersey and New York, Father Rutler was an Episcopal priest for nine years, and the youngest Episcopal rector in the country when he headed the Church of the Good Shepherd in Rosemont, Pennsylvania. He was received into the Catholic Church in 1979 and was sent to the North American College in Rome for seminary studies. His parents, Adolphe and Dorothy, both now deceased, were received into the Church in 1982 by Cardinal Cooke. Father Rutler graduated from Dartmouth, where he was a Rufus Choate Scholar, and took advanced degrees at the Johns Hopkins University and the General Theological Seminary. He holds several degrees from the Gregorian and Angelicum Universities in Rome, including the Pontifical Doctorate in Sacred Theology, and studied at the Institut Catholique in Paris. In England, in 1988, the University of Oxford awarded him the degree Master of Studies. From 1987 to 1989 he was regular preacher to the students, faculty, and townspeople of Oxford. Thomas More College awarded him an Honorary Doctorate in Humane Letters, and in 1996 Governor George W. Bush made him an Honorary Texan.

Father Rutler contributes to numerous scholarly and popular journals and has published 14 books on theology, history, cultural issues, and the lives of the saints, and also one book on sports, as a member of the U.S. Squash Racquets Association.

Of Related Interest

THE BAD CATHOLIC'S GUIDE TO WINE, WHISKEY, AND SONG

A Spirited Look at Catholic Life and Lore from Apocalypse to Zinfandel

Text by John Zmirak
and Recipes by Denise Matychowiak

View Catholic life from a unique perspective: through a shot glass. Starting with the wines, beers, and liquors made around the world by monks, the authors explore everything from Irish history to the "secrets" of the Knights Templar, with drinking games, food and cocktail recipes, and rollicking drinking songs. This A–Z dictionary of alcohol serves at once as a bartender's guide, a party planner, and a screwball catechism. Here you will discover:

• How vodka and whiskey were invented as medicine by monks • Catholic-safe replacements for most major profanities • Why the best ales are still made by Belgian Trappists • "Loopholes" to each of the Ten Commandments • How to translate the text of the Mass from Latin into Cockney • Drinking songs from around the world • The difference between Absolut Vodka and God •

0-8245-2411-X, paperback

crossroad

Of Related Interest

THE BAD CATHOLIC'S GUIDE TO GOOD LIVING

A Loving Look at the Lighter Side of the Catholic Faith, with Recipes for Feasts and Fun

Text by John Zmirak
and Recipes by Denise Matychowiak

Celebrate the Feast Days of the Saints — and don't forget your trampoline!

Jump right into this hilarious book on enjoying and celebrating Catholicism in a whole new way! Both a comical read and an indispensable resource for observing the Feast Days of the Saints, *The Bad Catholic's Guide to Good Living* is for anyone who is interested in celebrating the history and humor behind the Catholic Faith. Consisting of selected monthly historical sketches of the Feast Days, as well as suggested activities for celebration, this book serves as a must have for every happy Catholic! Written by a Catholic journalist and a four-star chef, it's an entertaining guide and guerilla catechism.

0-8245-2300-8, paperback

crossroad

Of Related Interest

Lorenzo Albacete
GOD AT THE RITZ
Attraction to Infinity

A Priest-Physicist Talks About
Science, Sex, Politics and Religion

A former NASA physicist and friend of Pope John
Paul II offers a thoughtful, timely, and often whim-
sical look at why religion still matters. Albacete
writes a column on religion for the *New York Times
Sunday Magazine*.

"Lorenzo Albacete is one of a kind, and so is *God at
the Ritz*. The book, like the monsignor, crackles with
humor, warmth, and intellectual excitement. Reading it is like having a stay-up-all-night, jump-out-of-
your-chair, have-another-double-espresso marathon
conversation with one of the world's most swash-
buckling talkers. Conversation, heck — this is a
papal bull session!"

—Hendrik Hertzberg,
The New Yorker Magazine

0-8245-1951-5, hardcover

crossroad

Of Related Interest

John J. Dietzen
CATHOLIC Q & A
*Answers to the Most Common Questions
about Catholicism*

Over 100,000 people have gone to their local Catholic bookstore or parish to buy *Catholic Q & A,* the authoritative question and answer book from Fr. John J. Dietzen, columnist for the Catholic News Service. Crossroad is delighted to take over publication of this Guildhall Publishers classic and introduce it to the general trade market for the first time.

Fr. Dietzen shows what the official church teaching is, as well as where church teaching is silent. This Crossroad edition will also carry the imprimatur, as earlier editions did.

ISBN 0-8245-2309-1, paperback

Check your local bookstore for availability.
To order directly from the publisher,
please call 1-800-707-0670 for Customer Service
or visit our Web site at *www.cpcbooks.com.*
For catalog orders, please send your request to the address below.

THE CROSSROAD PUBLISHING COMPANY
16 Penn Plaza, Suite 1550
New York, NY 10001

crossroad